Love Letter to a Conflicted Church

Love Letter to a Conflicted Church

Promise in Our Anger and Disagreements

RICHARD P. OLSON

RESOURCE *Publications* · Eugene, Oregon

LOVE LETTER TO A CONFLICTED CHURCH
Promise in Our Anger and Disagreements

Copyright © 2010 Richard P. Olson. All rights reserved. Except for brief quotations in critical publications or reviews, no part of this book may be reproduced in any manner without prior written permission from the publisher. Write: Permissions, Wipf and Stock Publishers, 199 W. 8th Ave., Suite 3, Eugene, OR 97401.

Resource Publications
An Imprint of Wipf and Stock Publishers
199 W. 8th Ave., Suite 3
Eugene, OR 97401

www.wipfandstock.com

ISBN 13: 978-1-60608-319-2

Manufactured in the U.S.A.

Grateful acknowledgment is given to Herald Press for permission to reprint selections from *Journey Toward Reconciliation* by John Paul Lederach (copyright © 1999); to Doubleday, a division of Random House, Inc. for permission to reprint selections from *No Future Without Forgiveness* by Desmond Tutu (copyright 1999); to Adrienne Kaufmann for permission to reprint her materials on "Search for Common Ground;" and to Bill Tammeus for permission to quote an excerpt from his essay, "Theologically Speaking, Modesty Would Help Us All," originally published in the Kansas City Star, August 4, 2001.

Unless otherwise indicated, all scripture quotations are from the New Revised Standard Version Bible, copyright © 1989, Division of Christian Education of the National Council of the Churches of Christ in the United States of America. Used by permission. All rights reserved.

Dedicated to the Church, particularly to those loveable, conflicted, purposeful, struggling, hopeful, caring, frustrating congregations where it has been my high calling and privilege to be pastor.

Contents

Preface / ix
Acknowledgments / xi

The Letter

"Dear members of a vital but painfully divided church..." / xiii

Reflection-Commentary on the Letter

Part One: Anger and Conflict Reconsidered

    Introduction: "Three Men and a Calf" / 3

1   The Gifts of Anger and Conflict / 10
2   The Redemptive Possibilities in Conflict / 21
3   Overcoming the Barriers to Creative Conflict / 32

Part Two: Revisiting the Bible for Perspectives on Conflict

4   Anger, Conflict, and Reconciliation in the Bible / 47
5   Beyond Conflict about the Bible: A Beginning Dialogue / 70
6   The Purpose of the Church: A Search for Biblical Priorities / 83

Part Three: Vistas of Change and Reconciliation

7   Parables of Hope and Promise / 95
8   Insights from Studies of Persons and Communities / 114
9   Further Aids to the Search from Christian Ethics and Theology / 131

10   What If—in Spite of All Our Efforts—We Are Still at Odds? / 144

11   A Healing Balm to the Nations: Activating Our Moral and Spiritual Imagination / 156

Resources for Congregations (and Other Entities) in Conflict / 173

Bibliography / 175

Preface

In this book I hope to open a conversation that, I am afraid, often does not happen until it is too late. This conversation is about anger and conflict, its place in our Christian lives and churches, and the possibilities for it being transformed and transformative.

While there are many excellent books on conflict in the church, I start earlier in the conversation and go some places other works do not go. The early start is to help you explore what you have been taught about anger-conflict, what are your present attitudes and beliefs about it, and why. Further, I consider how can anger-conflict be that helpful, redemptive experience.

The place I investigate that many others do not is how to learn from conflicts in the Bible. In particular, I initiate dialogue about our differences in Bible interpretation, certainly a place where many of our conflicts begin. Then a beginning exploration of biblical priorities for today and tomorrow's church is described.

Though not hiding my sometime pain and frustration, I also tell you what I have learned, how I am growing and hold before you the promise of a different way. Models of groups that transform conflict, information and perspective from Christian scholars, and more provide perspectives and strategies for creativity in conflict. At the end of each of the chapters, I offer some educative questions. These will help you carry the conversation further—with yourself and with others. My hope—extravagant, I am sure—is that this book is a multifaceted jewel. You can walk around it and see different possibilities of being creative, helpful, and effective with each other when conflicts come.

I hope that in addition to an individual read, this book will be explored by small groups, church boards, Sunday School classes, families, and groups of friends—anywhere where people care about each other but sometimes find it hard to discuss the difficult and divisive issues.

This is written out of a "lover's quarrel" with the church as it is, but an even deeper affection for the church and urgent prayer that it be all that it is intended to be in God's heart.

Acknowledgments

There are so many, who have shared this journey with me, learned with me and taught me. I especially thank the following:

- The several churches I have been privileged to serve as pastor or consultant.
- My colleagues on faculty and administration at Central Baptist Theological Seminary. They have read some of the chapters, critiqued, suggested, resourced, and improved them
- My students at Central, particularly those who participated in the "Conflict Transformation and Peace Building" class over the years.
- Dwight Lundgren, reconciliation services of American Baptist National Ministries, for subsidizing my study at Plowshares Institute and co-teaching Central students, but especially also teaching and enriching me.
- Friend and copy-editor Cynthia Jarrold, editor Christian Amondson and other supportive staff at Wipf and Stock Publishers.

The Letter

Dear members of a vital but painfully conflicted church:

Grace and peace to you from God whom we know in the Lord Jesus Christ.

I am grateful that I was called to serve as pastor with various churches for more than forty years. I am equally thankful that, in semi-retirement, it is my privilege to help prepare people for ministry with generations to come. There is nowhere I would rather have spent my life.

However, there has been a great agony in this. Opportunities for conflicts among church people abound. When we disagree, all too often we don't treat each other well. As a matter of fact, many church conflicts, whether in one church or among families of churches, frequently become downright ugly and hurtful. This is threatening our unity, to be sure. But deeper still, it is endangering our very life. In times past, some parts of the church have destroyed themselves by their relentless pursuit of their conflicts. How I pray that not happen to us!

I have personal reasons in my own history to be wary of church fights. For example, in the first congregation I served, a conflict that many persons thought quite minor undid much of the good we had accomplished in the years preceding.

There are many things we need to explore. We might begin by considering the possibility that anger and conflict, in addition to being natural and normal happenings, may also be a gift. But what kind of gift? Anger and conflict can help people clarify issues, clear the air, sense danger, confront injustice, and grow more purposeful. There is risk and trust when people face their anger and conflict openly. Some have discovered, to their amazement and awe, that they grow spiritually, and that while working on conflicts they are on holy ground.

Further, there are redemptive and transforming possibilities in conflict. Through conflict, a person can become more self-aware, articulate, and personally empowered. Not only that, one can learn to see the other as a human being, a child of God, and one with struggles and needs much like one's own. Indeed, redemption can happen in conflict when one obeys God and loves both neighbor and self.

I am aware, sisters and brothers, that these promises often have a hollow ring, for many of us have experienced anger and conflict so differently from that. There are wounds on our bodies and souls from past conflicts. We have also received well-intentioned but wrong interpretations of the Bible's teachings about conflict. And, we may have formed bad habits as regards anger and conflict. However, it need not stay that way. Ours is a gospel that invites us to begin again and is imbued with the power to change us.

And so, we turn to our Bible to hear the gospel of peace and peacemaking that is found there. Though there is much conflict and struggle recorded in our scriptures, we will also discover heart-warming stories of reconciliation within families, between brothers and sisters, in churches, and among tribes and nations. We will also find inspired prophetic visions of peace beyond anything the world has yet known.

The gospels describe our Lord addressing conflicts among his followers and seeking reconciliation and understanding even with his fiercest critics. The latter parts of the New Testament portray a church at work to heal its divisions so that the gospel might be clearly experienced. Most basically, the Bible points to God in Christ as our peace, the Source who unites us all.

Another important task is to understand each other's approach to and interpretation of scripture. Interpretation of the Bible is not only one of the places where we sometimes differ, it is also often the source of many of our other conflicts. So exploring ways of interpretation may be one of the topics where we will gain the most. It may clarify why we read the Bible as we do and also help us hear and understand another who reads the Bible differently. Out of this, we may find methods where we can jointly explore what is the Bible's message for us as we work on difficult issues.

As we come to such a place of mutual listening for God's voice within the Bible, there is a deep and profound question we must ask. What is the God of the Bible saying to the church about its mission in the twenty-first century? It may well be that a basic step to our deeper unity will be around that mission to which God calls us out of scripture.

Fellow saints and servants, there are also inspiring contemporary examples to guide and encourage us as we seek the path through conflict to a greater harmony in the church. Persons with radically different views have *looked for and discovered "Common Ground," holy ground. Others have discovered how to make church gatherings—boards and business meetings—"Worshipful Work." And leaders who began helping to heal the strife in the emerging nation of South Africa have gone many other places in the world helping persons work on divisive issues. They now offer the church their methods of "Peace Building and Conflict Transformation." The visions they had and the strategies they discovered may be used of God to inspire, guide, and stimulate us to find equally creative ways.*

We may also gain from the thoughts of contemporary leaders. Studies of how people interact as individuals and in communities provide food for thinking, acting, and relating. There are also truths to be learned from the Christian ethicists and theologians. We all are certain that God's will is a healthy, whole church on mission, and they may offer clues how this may be so.

But, you ask, what if after doing all this, we still have deep, intractable differences? Then we are called back to our basic beliefs—that God loves us, that Christ died and rose for us, and that those who believe are family of faith. Our conflict is with family of faith members, and this is our most basic reality. It is better to be respectful, considerate family members even with significant differences, than to be quarreling ones. Through the love that streams from the cross, there is always another way.

So, I urge you, stand by your basic convictions, but have a clear understanding of what is primary and what is secondary in our community of believers. In God's house, there are many abiding places, and we have room for many differences.

In closing, I remind you of that prayer Jesus offered for those of us who would come to believe through the word of his disciples. Jesus prayed "that they may all be one. As you, Father, are in me and I am in you, may they also be one in us so that the world may believe that you have sent me" (John 17:21).

A united, loving church will be a witness to the world that God sent Jesus. This healed and gracious church will have both the moral authority and the spiritual energy to be a caring presence in the troubled and conflicted spots in our world and society. What a joy it will be to be part of that healing!

And so, as did the great apostle Paul, I urge you to be of the same mind in the Lord. Loyal companions, who are not so directly involved in the issues, help those who are. For many of them have struggled for the gospel and their names are written in the book of life (Phil. 4:2-3).

"*The grace of* the Lord Jesus Christ be with your spirit" (Phil. 4:23). Amen!

PART ONE

Anger and Conflict Reconsidered

Introduction

Three Men and a Calf

> *I am grateful that in God's grace and providence, I was called to serve as pastor. . . . There is nowhere I would rather have spent my life.*
>
> *However, there has been a great agony in this. Opportunities for conflict among church people abound. When we disagree, all too often we don't treat each other all that well! As a matter of fact, many church conflicts, whether in one church or among families of churches, frequently become downright ugly and hurtful. This is threatening to our unity, to be sure. But deeper still, it is threatening our very life . . .*
>
> *I have personal reasons in my own history to be wary of church fights. For example, in the first congregation I served, a conflict that many persons thought quite minor undid much of the good we had accomplished in the years preceding . . .*

IT STARTED SO BEAUTIFULLY and ended so ugly, this story of three men and a calf.

I was a brand new pastor, fresh out of seminary, in my first congregation. The church consisted of 40–50 families, all farmers, and was located in a county seat town in a mid-western state.

I enjoyed working with the youth group, inviting them into the fun and the excitement of the Christian faith. Most of the young people were from established church families. However, one young man, Melvin was drawn into the group from a family on the fringe of church life. In time, Melvin became aware he was the only one in the youth group who had not professed Christ as Savior and been baptized. (In my denomination, babies are dedicated shortly after birth, and then baptized at a time of their choosing, preparation, and decision, usually similar to the time other denominations confirm young people.) He and I began talking about this possibility.

When I visited Melvin's parents, Howard and Jenny, and told them of these conversations, they said that they would also like to know more about their faith, and perhaps, they would like to be baptized, too. They also suggested I call on Jenny's parents, folks in their seventies, who had attended the church off and on for years but had never followed Christ in baptism. I did so, and this led to spiritual mentoring of three generations of this one family.

And so the joyous day came when I baptized a teenage young man (Melvin), with his parents (Howard and Jenny), and his grandparents all in the same service. It was the happiest day of my young ministry.

A few months later, while Howard was mowing alfalfa hay for another church member (Ronald), he came upon a stray calf. Howard put the calf in Ronald's pasture. They advertised it but insisted that people accurately identify its markings. Several people claimed it was their calf but could not precisely describe it. There had been a train wreck nearby, and some cattle had escaped. But when they called the railroad, they were told that all their livestock were either accounted for or already covered by insurance. Howard and Ronald concluded that good fortune had smiled upon them. They would raise and butcher it. Their frozen food lockers would be full for months to come.

However, another church member, Walter, insisted that the calf had strayed from his pasture and was his. Howard and Ronald were suspicious and doubtful—Walter's description of the calf was not entirely accurate. Further, Walter's pasture was more than two miles away and the calf would have had to come through multiple fences.

Then, one day, the calf disappeared from Ronald's pasture and wound up in Walter's. Walter insisted that the calf had made its own way back. Howard and Ronald were even more skeptical that the now larger calf had made its way through those several fences.

Each of the three felt he had some claim on that growing calf. All of them struggled financially. This calf would provide either much needed money or meat.

One Sunday after church, the three of them were standing outside, jawing about the calf. At that point, Walter's mother walked over to them and suggested. "Let's do this. I will pay for the calf's feed. When it is grown, we can sell it and give the money to the church." Neither Ronald nor Howard was very enthused, but they both reluctantly agreed.

Some months later at a church quarterly business meeting, Walter's mother made an announcement. She said that Walter and she had this calf that they decided to feed and then sell it and give the proceeds to the church. And so she presented a check to the treasurer. Ronald was present and was outraged at Gertrude's version of this story.

That was the first time I heard anything about the calf disagreement. I learned more the next day when I went to the grocery store where Ronald was a part time employee. He told me the whole story from his perspective and made clear that he had called Howard and told him the latest.

I didn't see anything that could be done right then. However, a few weeks later, I realized that Howard, Jenny, and Melvin had not been in church at all, an abrupt change in their attendance pattern. And so I went to see them.

I think they appreciated my coming. At the same time, they made it clear that they were sad, disillusioned, and absolutely through with the church. Howard told me, "Dick, I was a brand new Christian. I didn't know what to expect. But I didn't expect we'd spend our time fighting over a calf!"

This church had a reputation for a long history of feuding. I suppose that for Ronald and Walter, the calf conflict was probably just one more incident in a long series of not too important skirmishes.

Not so for this new family of young fragile Christians. They expected more of the church, and rightly so. They saw it all more clearly than any of the rest of us, and they were offended. Such actions shut down their enthusiasm for Christ and church. And though I made other calls and overtures in an attempt to heal those wounds, I never saw them in worship again.

The calf incident occurred over forty years ago, and it still haunts me. How I wish I had had something better to offer those people than their customary ways of dealing with each other so harshly. But what is that something better?

The better way is a different style of conflict that deals justly with people and their contested concerns. It upholds the dignity and worth of the contestants. This way embodies much needed new understandings of anger and conflict, and of many possible methods to deal with issues. We need to know how to hang with each other through long, seemingly unsolvable values and beliefs struggles. Of course, all of this is easier said than done. But this new and better way is needed even more now than then.

In the forty years since, I have never experienced another church fight over a calf. However, there have been struggles over many other things. Indeed, church conflicts have grown more widespread and vitriolic. Antagonism between congregation and pastor; friction between those of varying worship style preferences; differences as to who can be ordained; discord over theological, ideological, and life style issues—all this and more is part of the church scene today. Congregations self-destruct, and denominations are in peril of splitting, fracturing their local and world mission efforts. The inability of church people to deal with each other in constructive ways disillusions our young adults, mutes our witness, and calls it into question. "That is not the way you learned Christ!" (Eph. 4:20).

I am convinced that there are large numbers of church people, lovers of God and the church, people of good will. These people are on both sides of some of the hard issues facing the church, but they know that oneness in Christ is an all-important truth. And so, they dare to affirm, there are ways to deal with our conflicts—or live with them—as people of God. Though some are polarized in endless conflict from either extreme on issues, there is a healthy core in the middle. Revolution can come from the middle. I see myself as one of those persons in the middle, and if you are as well, I have some help to offer you.

I have been thinking, reflecting, and studying this matter of anger-conflict for many years, all the while searching for better ways of doing conflict, and, in so doing, have learned much from persons in many different disciplines. My purpose now is to tell you of these discoveries. I will provide some concepts, tools, and handles for living with the personal and church conflicts in your life as well as relate experiences and tell of conversations with wise people on this topic. There are thrilling stories of people overcoming their divisions all around the world. Today's church can be another of those stories.

There are at least two things I will *not* do in this book:

- I will not provide step by step process guides for resolving a personal, church, or denominational conflict. (The bibliography will provide a number of excellent resources, both books and agencies that do just that.)

- I will not speak directly about the issues that divide the church today. When these issues are mentioned, it will be to tell of folks who have learned to communicate with each other across those differences.

At the same time, there are two things I *will* do:

- I will try to stretch your mind on anger-conflict itself and on constructive engaging of these constant realities in our lives. Alternate perspectives, helpful insights, stories, and guidance from the Bible—this and more will be provided to aid your personal reflection and growth.
- I will provide a variety of resources for group discussion-exploration of this important theme. Each chapter has three components: (a) an excerpt from my opening letter to you; (b) food for thought; and (c) discussion questions.

The greatest value of this book may be for you to discuss it with another. You may have a friend or family member with whom you cannot discuss some topics. When a certain subject comes up, immediately the tension rises between the two of you.

It will be helpful for the two of you to covenant to read and discuss this book together. It will give you a chance to reflect on the *process* of conflict rather than its *content*. Further, it will invite the two of you to reflect on past experiences (with others), to identify what makes conflict difficult, and to develop new ways.

At the same time, this book might similarly enrich a variety of larger groups.

- It could be a church wide study group for classes and boards to help a church develop greater skillfulness in dealing with each other. This could be a general study or an investigation of how to deal with felt tensions in a congregation's life.
- It might provide a conversation guide for a dialogue group consisting of members of two or more churches, perhaps churches that are different in theology or ethnic or racial makeup. In this way, it may help open the door for more joint projects and deeper cooperation between Christian people in their mission to community and world.

- It could be helpful to judicatory or denominational leaders to help them gain perspectives and methods when consulting with churches or a resource to provide these churches.

Out of all of this, may a vision of a better way, of discoveries to make, lessons to learn, and of steps to take begin to emerge. If so, to God be the glory. Our scriptures proclaim that Christ loved the church and gave himself for us. We cannot treat with indifference that community he cared for at such cost.

Of course, I have opinions on some of these divisive issues. I hope that persons who are aware of these will not dismiss this book out of that knowledge. I promise not to press any of these viewpoints on anyone in these pages. At the same time, I won't disguise my passion for a healthier understanding of conflict and anger and its contribution to a renewed and revived church.

Occasionally at the church I attend, we sing a lovely new chorus—"Soften my heart, Lord, soften my heart."[1] The prayer chorus goes on to seek deliverance into Christ's compassion and tears. As I sing, my prayer includes my own struggling heart in conflicts and those with whom I disagree. As we begin this conversation, may it be that all our hearts are softened toward each other and to the leadership of our God.

QUESTIONS AND ACTIVITIES FOR GROUP REFLECTION

1. Do you have a story of a personal or church conflict to tell—either one that ended well or that did not? If so, pair up with another person and hear each other's stories.

2. What are your hopes and goals as you begin this group experience? Are they similar to what the author describes in this introduction and in the table of contents? If not, what other resources are needed for your group discussion? (Look at the bibliography at the end of the book.)

3. Are you aware of some other entity—perhaps a business, an organization, a family—that seems to do a better job handling conflict than does the typical church? If so, what could the

---

1. Graham Kendrick, "Soften My Heart," copyright 1988 by Make Way Music, found in *Renew! Songs and Hymns for Blended Worship* (Carol Stream: Hope Publishing Company, 1995) 223.

church learn from that other entity? (You might want to interview someone from that other organization or invite someone to visit with your group about their methods of dealing with conflict.)

4. What are your most successful strategies for dealing with conflict in your life?

5. What prayer support would you like from the group as regards existing or upcoming conflicts that you are facing?

1

The Gifts of Anger and Conflict

. . . As we reflect on these troubling matters, there are many things we need to explore. We might begin this journey by considering the possibility that anger and conflict, in addition to being natural and normal happenings, may also be a gift . . . but, what kind of gift? Anger and conflict can help people clarify issues, clear the air, sense danger, confront injustice, and grow more purposeful. There is risk and trust when people face their anger and conflict openly. Some have discovered, to their amazement and awe, that they grow spiritually, and that while working on conflicts they are on holy ground . . .

FOR YOUR PERSONAL OR GROUP WORSHIP

Scripture

He looked around at them with anger; he was grieved at their hardness of heart and he said to the man, "Stretch out your hand." (Mark 3:5)

Be angry but do not sin; do not let the sun go down on your anger, and do not make room for the devil. (Eph 4:26)

A Word to Ponder

Conflict presents us with choices that form our destiny, choices that both reflect and shape who we are as persons and communities. These choices go beyond the immediate issues in dispute. They mold our hearts and alter the world in which our children and grandchildren will live. In moments of conflict, we make long lasting decisions about the institutions and resources with which we construct our lives. Our deepest values shape and are shaped by our choices. Few moments bring together so many far-reaching choices as the moment of conflict.—Ronald S. Kraybill with Robert A. Evans and Alice Frazer Evans[1]

FOR YOUR THOUGHT AND REFLECTION

An Alternative View of Anger

We begin with a statement that, though strange, is both true and important. It is this—anger and conflict

- are entirely normal and natural,
- are gifts to us as individuals and as church,
- possess potential for great good and great growth, and
- present us with important ethical decisions and dilemmas.

A first response to this statement may be, "This is not what I was taught." A second may be, "This is not what I have experienced. Crabby people, violent people, unapproachable people have not made anger and conflict feel normal, natural, or gift to me." At very least, that opening statement may have to be qualified a good bit.

Like any other gift (money or sexuality, for example), the gifts of anger and conflict can be abused. If we are to address our tragic church divisions, we will need to be more accepting of anger-conflict, more comfortable with it, and more skilful in engaging it and challenging its excesses. Openness to this emotion is a place to start.

The gospels describe Jesus as a person who freely engaged in fitting anger and conflict. He was angry with people who would not discuss important issues with him (Mark 3:5), with religious leaders who missed the point of obedience to God (Matt 23:1–36), with an unresponsive Jerusalem (Matt 23:27–39, Luke 13:34–35), with moneychangers in the temple (Matt 21:11–13 and John 2:13–16). He confronted self-seeking disciples, would-be followers, and ungracious hosts. A fresh reading of the gospels will allow the follower of Christ to consider the possibility that for Jesus, anger and conflict were necessary and natural. As we watch his use and experience of anger and conflict, we see them as potential gifts, friends, and instruments for personal and church growth.

1. Kraybill and Evans, *Peace Skills*, 3.

We will look at Jesus's story of anger and conflict in much more detail in chapter 4.

Of course, it is not easy to feel good about one's anger. In his classic little book on this topic, Theodore Isaac Rubin notes, "Too often anger is not seen as basic or human. Anger is easily the most maligned . . . of feelings and responses." And yet, in spite of this, he goes on to suggest, "Feeling angry is a universal human phenomenon. It is as basic as feeling hungry, lonely, loving, or tired. The capacity to feel angry and to respond in some way to that feeling is in us from birth."[2]

No one, certainly not Dr. Rubin, would contend that this is a gift without its dangers. Unrecognized, suppressed, misdirected anger can be damaging to one's own physical and mental health and to one's important relationships. It is a gift that cries out for recognition; if not afforded that recognition, it can sting us!

Once recognized, it can be so enriching to our lives. Audre Lorde comments, "Anger is loaded with information and energy . . . [and is] an important source of empowerment."[3]

Harriet Lerner enumerates these gifts of anger so well—

> Anger is a signal, and one worth listening to. Our anger may be a message that we are being hurt, that our rights are being violated, that our needs or wants are not being adequately met, or simply that something is not right. Our anger may tell us that we are not addressing an important emotional issue in our lives, or that too much of our self—our beliefs, values, desires, or ambitions—is being compromised in a relationship. Our anger may be a signal that we are doing more and giving more than we can comfortably do or give. Or our anger may warn us that others are doing too much for us, at the expense of our own competence and growth. Just as physical pain tells us to take our hand off the hot stove, the pain of our anger preserves the very integrity of our self. Our anger can motivate us to say "no" to the ways in which we are defined by others and "yes" to the dictates of our own inner self.[4]

Counselors have long noted that anger is almost always the second emotion. There is a basic emotion—hurt or fear or pain, for example— that comes first. Anger comes second and is what we express rather than

---

2. Rubin, *The Angry Book*, 11, 17.
3. Lordre, quoted in Saucy, *The Gift of Anger*, 113.
4. Lerner, *The Dance of Anger*, 1.

the primary emotion. Thus, as Lerner points out, a gift of anger is to alert us to what are the primary feelings.

Greater self-awareness, more zest for living, sensitivity to inner hurts and relationships that need attention, more inner freedom—all of this and more can come from an acceptance and recognition of anger in one's life.

Of course, these benefits do not come automatically. Quite often, if I am to gain from this greater self-awareness, I need to carry on a conversation with the person or organization with whom I am angry. Quite possibly this will lead to conflict.

An Alternative View of Conflict

Conflict is the other of the gifts we are exploring in this chapter. While anger is the inner, personal experience, conflict is the outer, relational expression. Like anger, conflict is a normal experience in human life. Abraham Lincoln once commented that the situation of the world could be seen in his two sons. He had three walnuts and each son wanted two!

That is pretty normal, as are most of our conflicts. We live in marriages, families, churches, communities where our needs compete, things not to our liking often happen, and there are differences over troubling issues. When two or more parties each seek their best interest, there will be conflict. If natural and inevitable, conflict need not be evil, wrong, or destructive. Since conflict is normal, we can be more relaxed about those with whom we have conflicts.[5] Also, we can be free to let the conflict unfold.

Why is there anger and conflict in the world? Where did it come from? John Paul Lederach invites us to consider the opening chapters of Genesis. There is beautiful, delightfully chaotic creation, and there are Adam and Eve, two free human beings, each created in the image of God naming the animals.

> As Adam and Eve were naming the animals and plants, feeding themselves, filling the earth, and being fruitful and multiplying, can you imagine that they went about their tasks without disagreement and argument? Both were created in the image of God. Each was an individual, and each had freedom. Can you

---

5. Kraybill and Evans, 9.

really imagine that they never argued or disagreed? How utterly boring, if that were the case![6]

Lederach goes on to suggest that this imaginative peek is a "Genesis window" into conflict—it is, quite probably, pre-fall. This view gives at least a biblical hint that conflict is natural, contrary to the frequent opinion that conflict is sinful. "By the very way we are created, conflict will be a part of our ongoing human experience."[7]

Andrew Lester concurs. He points out that the capacity for anger is deeply rooted in our physicality, including our senses and brain chemistry. The creation accounts tell us that God (whom the Bible portrays as having the capacity for emotions) created us in God's image (including emotions). Further, God created us with the capacity for anger before the fall, and looked on all of God's creation—including humans with human emotions—and pronounced it very good![8]

As with anger, conflict's contributions to us are not automatic. Things can go wrong in conflict. And yet, quite often, avoiding conflict leads to worse consequences than a botched attempt to face it and work on it.

I learned some of the values of conflict from a man named Fritz. Fritz's wife and children were practicing Roman Catholics. He came to the church I served by himself, came faithfully, sang in the choir, and served on the board of deacons. At those board meetings, whenever I offered a suggestion or presented a new vision or plan, Fritz would resist. He would let his skepticism show, ask hard questions, and he would stir up questions from others on the board as well. There wasn't meanness or nastiness in his objections, just consistency and predictability. The result was that as a board we moved slowly. We selected just a few of my suggested efforts and rejected others. Then we improved on the ones we chose and made them more of a whole board project.

In my youthful impatience, I did not see this at the time. However, time and Fritz's final comment to me helped me understand. When I completed my time of service at that church, as Fritz was saying goodbye, he advised me, "Dick, always have a 'no man' on every board." (A "no woman" will do just fine.) Fritz's strategy was deliberate—make the

---

6. Lederach, *The Journey Toward Reconciliation*, 116–17.
7. Ibid.
8. Lester, *The Angry Christian,* 169–77.

process better by constant, low key, good-natured conflict and questioning. God bless him!

Anger and Conflict's Potential Gifts

What are some of the specific benefits that can come from this gift called conflict? There are many.

We start with the benefits to one-on-one relationships such as friendship or marriage. (These often carry over to larger groups and organizations, as well.) Some years ago, marriage therapist George Bach, weary of dealing with failing marriages, decided he would find, interview, and learn from some strong, healthy marriages. And so, when at social gatherings or visiting with counseling colleagues, he asked folks if they knew of any really strong marriages. He would get the names and addresses of couples mentioned, call, and ask to interview them.

Out of this research he made two discoveries. One was that sadly, many marriages that had a good public image were in truth not very strong. He spoke of them as "card-house marriages"—relationships with a fake front that were instead very shaky. The other was that in the few really healthy marriages he found, they "argued constantly. They thought conflict was as natural as eating."[9]

While more recent marriage research does not concur that all strong marriages are constantly fighting, there are substantial benefits for those who accept conflict as normal and learn to do it well.

Pastor and social worker Daniel Langford suggests at least four valuable things about conflict in a marriage or family. For one, conflict provokes communication. (At least it can.) When two or more people have a problem, whether with each other or not, the issue needs to be addressed. This can only be done through communication. (Though goodness knows married partners have tried countless other ways.) If the conflict stimulates deeper, more accurate, and more honest communication, it has served well.

Closely related is his second suggestion, that conflict helps persons to become better acquainted. It can contribute to greater intimacy. Couples have a relationship journey. This journey begins with mutual attraction and enjoyment, when it seems they have everything in common. As the relationship goes on, each discovers they have some differ-

---

9. Bach and Wyden, *The Intimate Enemy*, 47–48.

ences. However, they may suppress these for a while. Eventually, these differences cannot be avoided any longer. Some conflict issue arises that needs to be faced, negotiated, and resolved. Then, indeed, both know the other better after that. Conflicts have helped Daniel and his wife, Diana, know and understand each other better and love each other more fully.

Third, conflict gives occasion and grants permission to express and release pent-up emotions. The freedom to express emotions in an intimate relationship is vital to developing and maintaining closeness. On the other hand, if one denies the anger and runs away from the conflict, it may have the detrimental effect of blocking all of the other emotions. Each emotion adds zest and color to the lives of individuals and relationships.

While this benefit is true, it needs to be stated accurately and carefully. Marriage therapists are increasingly discovering that it is not necessarily helpful to "let it all hang out." It is counterproductive to express one's anger indiscriminately and endlessly. At the same time, recognition of anger and clarity about the conflict issue at stake are vital to the health of any relationship.

And fourth, conflict identifies and clarifies problems. In any situation, diagnosis is important. An important diagnostic tool for a couple to know how they are doing is to pay attention to their anger, their complaints, and their conflicts. These are reliable clues as to how a good relationship can become even better rather than deteriorate. (Of course, they should also pay attention to their delights, joys, humor, and laughter in the relationship, as well.) In this connection, Langford quotes John Bradshaw, "The capacity for conflict is a mark of intimacy and a mark of a healthy family. Good healthy conflict is a kind of contact."[10]

But we have only begun to note the benefits that this gift of conflict can bring. Another is this—since the experience of conflict is frequent and normal, engaging in it can increase our skill and comfort level. This in turn can encourage our partners in family and church to raise worthy issues for consideration and negotiation, as Fritz did.

A church conflict need not be a new, strange, and feared event. Indeed Ronald Kraybill has suggested that if churches want fewer divi-

---

10. Langford, *The Pastor's Family,* 62–65. He is quoting John Bradshaw, *The Family,* 52–53.

sive and church-splitting conflicts, they should encourage more everyday disagreements in their congregational life.[11]

George W. Bullard, Jr. not only concurs, but puts it even more strongly. "Every congregation needs a little conflict," he asserts. Why? "Because congregations without conflict are dead or dying." He goes on to list seven reasons that absence of what he calls "a healthy intensity of conflict" hampers the life of a church:

1. "Congregations without a healthy intensity of conflict do not have passion around their mission, purpose, and vision." Tension and conflict around these vital issues is helpful in defining them.

2. "Congregations without a healthy intensity of conflict do not have clear beliefs and core values."

3. "Congregations without a healthy intensity of conflict function in an avoidance lifestyle." The very fear of conflict stands in the way of facing important topics.

4. "Congregations without a healthy intensity of conflict make shallow decisions that come from a group-think mentality." There is a sense that leaders are not to be questioned. Harmony and homogeneity is preferred to diversity and innovation.

5. "Congregations without a healthy intensity of conflict do not have the opportunity to learn how to handle decision making around complex issues and thus how to handle transitional and unhealthy conflict when it is experienced."

6. "Congregations without a healthy intensity of conflict do not learn how to deep conflict from escalating to an unhealthy intensity." Or, to put it still another way,

7. "Congregations without a healthy intensity of conflict do not take many risks because they are afraid taking risks will create conflict they cannot handle." Thus, such churches do not reach their full kingdom potential.[12]

---

11. Cited by Lederach, 144.
12. George W. Bullard, Jr., *Every Congregation Needs a Little Conflict*, 8–9.

It is true that in conflict, a church can be energized. When there are no issues, problems, great causes to be explored, little change will happen. When there is a threat, a problem, an issue, persons will mobilize to meet the challenge.

William Willimon recalls serving a congregation in decline. It was his difficult responsibility to confront them with the problem, that unless things changed drastically, that church would be gone in a decade or two. While this necessary information could have discouraged and depleted some congregations, this congregation heard it as a call to mobilization. They used their vision and creativity to meet the threat of extinction. Visitation, greeters, remodeling, new groups, and classes all came forth from the prophetic confrontation by their pastor.

This leads him to agree that a congregation needs, perhaps even enjoys, a certain amount of tension and conflict, and will welcome such occasional controversial leadership from their pulpit. The pastor will hear a few complaints about a controversial sermon. At the same time, there are others longing for excitement and a new challenge. While they should not create conflict where none need exist, pastors and other church leaders are wise to invite the church into the new life that sometimes awaits when confronted with large questions and overwhelming challenges—and the inevitable conflict that goes with such experiences.[13]

Further still, as Andrew Lester notes, anger (and the corresponding conflict) is "spiritual ally." He recalls early church father Evagius Ponticus who encouraged anger when tempted as a chief motivator in our struggle against sin. Evagrius went so far as to suggest that "uttering angry words can be creative in freeing us to pray!"[14] There are a number of ways in which anger-conflict can be spiritual ally. Anger can be a stimulus to hope—the sense that things can be different. Similarly, it can stir us up to courage. "Anger can give us the energy and the willingness to speak up, speak out, march, vote, protest, refuse to participate, resist evil, and blow the whistle. Anger provides courage. . . ."[15] Also, anger can help a person establish boundaries for oneself and recover a sense of self-identity and worth. Lester points out further that anger is useful as "idol detector." We become angry when those items we have put at the center of our life are threatened. This may be other persons and their opinions, habits or

13. Willimon, *Preaching About Conflict in the Church*, 15–18.
14. Lester, 124. The quote is in Lester's words, paraphrasing Evagrius.
15. Ibid., 193.

addictions (such as smoking) or sports teams, for example. Any of these can become an attachment that has been allowed to gain strength of meaning and importance that should be reserved for God. Our anger may be the detecting device that tells us this is so.[16]

To look at this from a slightly different angle, conflict itself has a spiritual dimension in that it is a revelatory event. When conflict or other challenge comes, persons and churches are called to be in touch with their resources of faith. How does the Bible illumine this time? Where is God in this? What is the Spirit saying? How does God view the persons who are on the other side of this conflict?

At first, we may feel blank and panicky when confronted with conflict and what seems to be our own spiritual emptiness in the face of it. And yet, the Christian faith has undergirded many persons in the face of such challenges. With eyes of faith, we wait upon the Lord, trusting it shall be so.

As Carolyn Schrock-Shenk notes, part of this revelation is of myself. Without conflict, we tend to keep ourselves carefully hidden from God, self, and others. She suggests, "Struggling through conflict can make us vulnerable, sharpen our senses, help us see our own inadequacy and narrow mindedness, and open us to God and to others in new ways."[17]

Indeed, this is the witness of many of the Psalms. The Psalmist cries out to God one's lament, searching, doubts, accusations. (See, for example Ps 3:1–2 and Ps 10:1–13.) The writer of the Psalms is totally transparent before God. The conflict and the honesty about it do not destroy the relationship with God. Rather, such a struggle strengthens the bond of knowing as sometimes (not always) the psalmist comes to new truth and a fresh experience of God (Ps 3:3–8, 10:14–18).

John Paul Lederach, who works in many difficult and dangerous conflict mediation situations, writes, "Deep conflicts are stressful and painful. At worst, they are violent and destructive. Yet at the same time, they create some of the most intense spiritual encounters we experience. Conflict opens a path, a holy path toward revelation and reconciliation."[18]

---

16. Ibid., 200–201.
17. Schrock-Shenk and Ressler, eds., *Making Peace With Conflict,* 26–27 (Schrock-Shenk's personally written introduction to this anthology).
18. Lederach, 14.

If such possibilities and more are available to us in anger and conflict, and if our experience with these so far has been so different from that, what then? Where is the road, and what is the guidance to help us move from hurtful conflict to transforming conflict? That will be our topic in the next chapter.

QUESTIONS AND ACTIVITIES FOR GROUP REFLECTION

1. I suggest a number of benefits that can come from anger and conflict. List them. Which of these have you experienced?

2. Of this list of possible benefits from anger-conflict, which do you accept? Which do you question?

3. What has been your best experience of conflict? What gain or growth did you experience as a part of it?

4. What has been your worst experience of anger or conflict? In the light of this chapter, what will you do differently the next time you face a similar experience?

5. I make several assertions and list supporting passages about anger and conflict in Jesus's life. How does this strike you? Is the information accurate and true?

6. What was your opinion on anger and conflict when you started reading this chapter? What is it now? If you are skeptical, what will it take to convince you?

2

The Redemptive Possibilities in Conflict

. . . Further, there are redemptive and transforming possibilities in conflict. Through conflict a person can become more self aware, articulate, and personally empowered. Not only that—one can learn to see the other as a human being, a child of God, one with struggles and needs much like one's own. Indeed, redemption can happen in conflict when one obeys Jesus to love both neighbor and self . . .

FOR YOUR PERSONAL OR GROUP WORSHIP

Scripture

. . . I made up my mind not to make you another painful visit. For if I cause you pain, who is there to make me glad but the one whom I have pained. And I wrote as I did, so that when I came, I might not suffer pain from those who should have made me rejoice; for I am confident about all of you, that my joy would be the joy of all of you. For I wrote you out of much distress and anguish of heart and with many tears, not to cause you pain, but to let you know the abundant love I have for you. But if anyone has caused pain, he has caused it not to me, but to some extent—not to exaggerate it—to all of you. This punishment by the majority is enough for such a person; so now instead you should forgive and console him, so that he may not be overcome by excessive sorrow.

For even if I made you sorry with my letter, I do not regret it (though I did regret it, for I see I grieved you with that letter, though only briefly). Now I rejoice, not because you were grieved, but because your grief led to repentance; for you felt a godly grief, so that you were not harmed in any way by us. (2 Cor 2:1–7, 7:8–9)

A Word to Ponder

> A robust spirituality of anger faces a daunting future: overcoming our amnesia of irascible prophets and an angry Jesus; admitting conflict as a necessary dynamic in our religious lives; disbelieving that violence can remedy our differences; recrafting civility as a political virtue; reinvigorating the ancient virtues of courage and temperance. Short of such a renaissance, we will be left with a moribund religious tradition of anger as a deadly sin and a cultural heritage of violence as the ordinary and acceptable voice of anger. (James D. Whitehead and Evelyn Eaton Whitehead)[1]

FOR YOUR THOUGHT AND REFLECTION

When I think of the redemptive possibilities of conflict, I recall two profound experiences in my own life.

The first happened when I was twenty years old, a college student, state president of my denominational youth fellowship. The staff member who advised our youth organization was a man named Ray. I liked Ray; he was full of fun and life, always kind, but sometimes necessarily firm. I had lost my father as a child and never had a big brother. Though I never allowed anyone to fill either of those voids, I did somehow invite Ray to come as close as I had allowed any older male. That he thought highly of me and often publicly praised me was all the better. His office and my college were just a block apart, and so I would drop by often. I might have some work of our organization to discuss, but I just liked to be with him.

Sometimes, we traveled to out of town functions together, Ray and his wife in the front seat, my girlfriend (later fiancée and wife) and I in the back. We'd have a good time on those trips. Occasionally my girlfriend and I would do a little (I hoped discrete) necking on the journey back home.

Then, one day, to my shock and great hurt, I heard from someone else that Ray had criticized my behavior! I brooded about this until I could stand it no longer. And so I went to his office.

---

1. James D. Whitehead and Evelyn Eaton Whitehead, *Shadows of the Heart: A Spirituality of Negative Emotions,* 101.

I had some excuse for going and transacted that bit of business quickly. Then with a huge chip on my shoulder, I blurted out, "I hear you have some criticisms of me. I'd like to hear them."

Ray was nearly twice my age, but he treated me with dignity and respect. He admitted, that when questioned, he had said some things to others he should have said to me. He apologized and asked my forgiveness. He spoke of how much we had in common, including our passion for the women we love. Then he went on to say what he should have said to me first—that places of respect and leadership (like my being state youth president) carried responsibilities of modeling high standards and behavior. He spoke of a few times—not just in the back seat of his car—when he felt I could have been more careful about what I was communicating to the youth I was leading by the way I conducted myself with the woman I loved.

I accepted his apology and forgave. In addition, I listened to his hard truth and tried to do better. Most of all, I was relieved that this conflict did not destroy our relationship. Instead, I vaguely sensed, it was the occasion for moving on to something better.

This was in the days before I hugged men, but our long firm handshake was just as good. The friendship deepened and continued. Ray was one of the ministers at our wedding, a frequent guest in our home.

The second experience was with a person, let's call him John. I was a pastor in a university community in the west. One day my mail included a mass mailing from John to all pastors in the city. John was director for the local pro-life organization, and the invitation was to come see a new film sponsored by his organization and then discuss it afterward.

I had a schedule conflict, and so on the RSVP card, I wrote that I could not come, was of a different viewpoint, but would come and see his film if it were scheduled another time. I thought that would be the end of it. However, in a few days, I had a phone call from John. He said if I had a projector, he would come with the film, and we—just the two of us—could view and discuss it together at a time of my convenience.

We set a time and met, cordially, if somewhat stiffly. Almost immediately we watched the film. When it ended, there was silence. Then, John asked me, "What did you think of the film and its message?" At first, I attacked what I considered some of the unfair propaganda in the film. He was not distracted by that but pushed me to confront the essential message within. This led to a deep and frank discussion of why we held the positions we did, of our uneasiness with some parts of our position, of our search for a way to deal with this tragic conflict. Then we rewound the film and he left.

John had the kindness and courtesy to write me a follow up letter. I wish I still had it, but I remember what he said. "You did not convince me of your position, and I did not expect you to. I did not convince you of my position, and I did not expect to. But you took me more seriously than many that share my position. And for that, I thank you." John was a person of strong convictions and of equally strong good will. As he said, he did not change my opinion. However, he did something even more valuable; he permanently altered the way I would think about those with whom I differ on this subject. I thank him for modeling how conflict can be transformed (and transformative) even when there is incomplete resolution.

I don't have as many of these stories to tell as I would like, and I wonder why. Both of these experiences involved discomfort and risk. However, if the efforts to understand had failed, we would have been no worse off than when we began. The rewards from risking the confrontation were tremendous! From your stories and mine, perhaps we can learn more about the redemptive possibilities in conflict.

Attitudes and Expectations about Conflict

Those who work in this field point out that there are a number of attitudes and expectations about conflict. Further, what we expect and hope to achieve going into a conflict may well influence what happens and what comes out. So let's take a look at the variety of approaches.[2]

Some prefer and believe it is most helpful to engage in *conflict avoidance*, or at least *conflict postponement*. There is an adage that time heals all wounds, and some feel this applies to conflict. Leave it alone and it will go away. There is a partial truth here. Some hurts and strains seem very important when they happen, but in perspective seem much less so. The trouble with this position is that we are not always wise enough to

---

2. In the following section, I will be combining, summarizing, paraphrasing, and interpreting the thoughts of the following: Robert A. Baruch Bush and Joseph P. Folger, *The Promise of Mediation*; Ronald S. Kraybill with Robert A. Evans and Alice Frazer Evans. *Peace Skills: A Manual for Community Mediators*; and Carolyn Schrock-Shenk and Lawrence Ressler (eds). *Making Peace With Conflict*.

The Redemptive Possibilities in Conflict

recognize what differences, strains, and struggles are important enough to be given careful attention, and which differences are not.

Another approach is *conflict prevention*. Anticipate the issues and problems, and invite participation in the planning. Design the strategy and organization so well that there need be no conflict. While this is a worthy goal, it also needs at least two cautions. One caution is that it is naïve to think this is entirely possible. There will be unanticipated issues, problems, needs, and some conflict is inevitable in the resolving of these. The other caution is that in seeking conflict prevention, folks should not ignore the realities of injustice that often underlie conflict. Sometimes, in the interest of justice, conflict needs to be increased, not prevented.

Conflict resolution is another possible goal. This is a term that was coined by early leaders in mediation. It expresses the hope that issues can be clearly identified, acceptable compromises discovered, and agreement reached. The term implies that conflict can be finished, wrapped up, put behind. While this is certainly part of what is wanted, it ignores other parts—people, their struggles, their relationships.

Conflict management is a later term suggested by community mediators. With similar goals to conflict resolution, this viewpoint also looks for ways of "keeping the lid on." Conflict and the ways we express it should be kept within reasonable and acceptable parameters. It should be carried on a civil manner. These are things that all who go into conflict hope for. At the same time, the concept is open to question. Kraybill and Evans ask, "But can anyone really 'manage' conflict? Can geologists 'manage' Mount Vesuvius? Must we 'manage' the sun to benefit from solar energy?"[3]

As of late, some community mediators have been speaking of a new, more comprehensive goal—*conflict transformation*. "Conflict resolution" focuses mostly on the problem, the issue at stake, and gives attention to the resolution of that problem. "Conflict management" focuses on the process, the methods, and the procedures to work through the conflict, hopefully in an orderly fashion. While "conflict transformation" does not ignore either issues or process, it focuses more directly on the people involved, their relationship with each other, and on what happens to them as they experience the conflict.[4] I believe that it is in

---

3. Kraybill and Evans, 4.
4. Schrock-Shenk and Ressler, 35.

this emphasis, most of all, that creative and redemptive possibilities in conflict can be found.

All of us who enter into conflict can come out of it changed for the better! One thing is certain; we will come out of a conflict changed. Those who study this field have noted that in the Chinese language, the term for crisis and for conflict is the same term. They have also noted that this term includes two words, "danger" and "opportunity." A crisis is a danger that is also an opportunity; it is a dangerous opportunity.

Crisis counselors know that when we walk with a person through a crisis, the goal is not simply coping, survival, business as usual when the crisis is over. Rather, the crisis interrupts one's usual way of living and coping. (If those methods were sufficient, there would not have been a crisis!) If a person is open to what the experience is telling one, s/he can leave it with new strengths, fresh vision, a new and different way of living.[5]

Pastoral counseling pioneer Howard Clinebell often offered the equation "caring plus confrontation equals change." That should probably be qualified a bit, that when one person offers both caring and confrontation to another, that person at least will have increased openness to the possibility of change. While Clinebell was thinking of the counseling or other caring relationship, his insight speaks to those who seek to learn and gain from their conflicts as well.

All of this relates to some practical wisdom that floats among married couples. One or both partners may be upset or uncomfortable about things in the relationship, but may be hesitant to raise them, fearful of the struggle that will emerge. The wisdom is this: "Oh, go ahead and have that fight. It's so much fun to make up!" In the conflict, they may or may not resolve the issue. But, if the advice is true and applies, they rediscover their hunger for communion, for closeness, for touching and being held by each other. And that is one aspect of transforming conflict.

Robert A. Baruch Bush and Joseph P. Folger write, ". . . the most important goal [in conflict mediation] is *engendering moral growth* and *transforming human character*, toward both *greater strength* and *greater compassion*."[6] They contend that these qualities can emerge from a conflict in such significant measure that a solution to the issue, while

---

5. See, for example, Howard W. Stone, *Crisis Counseling,* 28–30.
6. Bush and Folger, 27. The emphasis in italicized letters is mine.

always desirable is secondary and almost anticlimactic. (That beautifully describes what happened to me in my conflict with John.)

Empowerment

The terms they use for the possible transformation are *empowerment* and *recognition*. Let's consider these in turn.

There are many ways that empowerment can happen to the parties in a conflict.

- There may be empowerment as regard to *goals*, a clearer understanding of what is important to one, and why one holds to these goals.
- There may be empowerment as to *options*, the recognition of a wider range of choices, processes and methods one can choose, accept, or reject.
- There may be empowerment of *skills*, as one learns how better to listen, communicate, analyze issues, present one's own arguments, brainstorm and evaluate possible solutions.
- There may be empowerment as to *resources* as one becomes aware that one has the means to achieve some goals and objectives, has support from others, and/or has the "know how" to implement solutions not previously considered.
- There may be empowerment as to *decision making*, as one increasingly becomes able to assess the strengths and weaknesses of one's own arguments and the other's, as well as the advantages and disadvantages of possible solutions, and then makes decisions in light of this reasoning.[7]

Growing stronger and clearer as regards goals, options, skills, resources, and decision-making, that, and more, is what they mean by empowerment. Conflicts can be vital learning and growing experiences. Individuals and groups can emerge all the stronger from such an experience.

---

7. Ibid., 85–87.

Recognition

The second of the transforming goals for conflict is recognition. That is, recognition of the other, the person or group with whom one has the conflict. Early in a conflict, this is not easy. There may be past history, antagonisms, and hurts to overcome. Individuals or groups may feel threatened, attacked, victimized. They may be defensive, suspicious, and hostile.

Starting from this point, it is surely a mark of transforming growth when there can begin to emerge some openness, attention, sympathy, response to the situation of the other. Sometimes a skilled, neutral mediator will be needed to help this begin to emerge. However, this is another of the redemptive possibilities, one needed to balance the growth through recognition. Again, Bush and Folger note several aspects of recognition.

- It might begin with *consideration* of giving recognition, the awareness that one can reflect not only on one's own, but the other's struggle, that one is secure enough to reflect both on what oneself and the other is going through.
- It might continue with the *desire* for giving recognition. There may be the awareness that not only is one able; one also desires to acknowledge some of the pain and struggle of the other.
- A further step is giving recognition in *thought*. One consciously engages in absorbing new information about the life, pressures, struggles, and issues of the other; in turn one may be able to reinterpret past actions and understand why the other did what s/he did. At such times, perhaps "the light goes on."
- Still another step is giving recognition in *words*. The person openly acknowledges his or her changed perspective, either to the mediator or to the other contending party. Along with the statement of how one sees things in a new way, there may be an apology of some kind.
- And then, there may be yet another step, giving recognition in *actions*. As the parties move toward some resolution, one may offer to make some concrete accommodations to the other, to take specific steps that bring deeper community, resolution, and

mutual acceptance.[8] The actions might include some kind of ritual that is an expression of and a seal upon the agreements and covenants made. For example, the parties might have a cup of coffee or a meal together, or a prayer or worship service, or an embrace.

Recognition of the other in consideration, desire, thought, words, actions—that may seem far removed from how most people experience conflict. Whatever may happen, parties should offer only the recognition they can genuinely give.

Empowerment of parties can be achieved in all conflicts. Recognition may or may not happen. If it does, it may start in such small doses that it takes a skilled observer to recognize it and then name it and encourage it. It may wax and wane during the negotiations around a conflict. However, recognition should always be in mind as a transforming possibility and goal.

Spiritual-Theological Dimensions

Up to now, I have been offering you the insights of scholars and practitioners of conflict mediation. Their language is largely secular. However, we need to note that the words "empowerment" and "recognition" are terms for closely related spiritual goals of conflict. Indeed these words-ideas translate readily into spiritual concepts.

Remember that our Lord commanded us to love our neighbors as ourselves (Matt 22:39). In empowerment, I obey one part of that command, to love myself. I listen carefully and deeply to my heart, to my feelings, hopes, needs, values, commitments. I look for the Spirit of God within me.

In recognition, I obey the other part of Jesus's command, to love neighbor. I listen equally deeply to the heart of another and the Spirit of God in that person. I recognize that person as child of God, image of God, neighbor, brother-sister for whom Christ died. As Carolyn Schrock-Shenk notes, "Neither of these are easy tasks in the presence of conflict, precisely because we tend to be weak and self-absorbed, unable to hear our own hearts or the heart of another. Squarely in the midst of

---

8. Ibid., 89–91.

these tendencies, however, lies the powerful transformative potential of conflict."[9]

David R. Sawyer walks even deeper into the theological dimension of religious conflict. The title of his book, *Hope in Conflict: Discovering Wisdom in Congregational Turmoil*, expresses his basic and fascinating thesis. He prefers the term "conflict utilization." By that term, he says:

> I mean to suggest that the conflict itself presents an opportunity to imagine what God desires for the congregation's future. The hopeful leader sees the experience of conflict as an opportunity to unravel the clues in the deeper life of a congregation and to ask where God is working or trying to work in their midst. We can make the most of a conflict situation if we approach it as a mysterious and hopeful moment in the life of the congregation that requires our best spiritual, intellectual, and practical skills.[10]

Sawyer notes that church conflicts are situations where the theological qualities of love and hope are most needed and most helpful. He advises, "Listening for the deep message of goodness and health in the church, and loving the church and its members even at their most unlovely, can make a difference." Further, "In most conflicts, a sense of hope is more important than the techniques for conflict management, or communication skills, although those are also useful."[11] When conflict arises, it is not occasion for despair. Rather it is an opportunity for revelation and renewal. What is God saying and what is God calling to the church in this conflict? When those questions and answers are discerned, it approaches the ultimate in recognition and empowerment!

At the beginning of this chapter, I told you of two rich experiences of conflict and reconciliation in my life. Both of those encounters took place before I had learned as much about conflict as I know now. We just muddled through. As I look at those experiences in the light of this chapter, I can see in both situations that each party grew both in empowerment and in recognition. We both loved the neighbor before us and ourselves more deeply than before we had engaged in the conflict.

All that is true, and it is helpful, but it does not tell all. When I think of those conflict experiences I remember them as deeply mystical and spiritual. I had read the Bible about reconciliation, had studied

---

9. Schrock-Shenk and Ressler, 36.
10. David Sawyer, *Hope in Conflict*, 9.
11. Ibid.

theological texts and preached sermons on it. But, on those occasions of encounter, reconciliation became more deeply a part of me and of the good news I proclaim. All these years later, I feel a lump in my throat and breathe a prayer of thanksgiving for such people and such experiences.

From deep within my own journey I heartily affirm what was hinted at the end of the previous chapter. I now dare to believe that whenever Christians with great differences attempt to reach out to each other with respect and searching for understanding, we are, indeed, standing on holy ground.

QUESTIONS AND ACTIVITIES FOR GROUP REFLECTION

1. In this chapter is mentioned various ways of dealing with conflict—avoidance, postponement, prevention, resolution, management, transformation. To which of these approaches do you seem to be drawn when conflict seems about to happen? Do you know why? Which of the approaches do you prefer? Are these different from the ones you most often use?

2. At the end of chapter one, you were asked to recall your best experience of conflict. If you did so, call that experience to mind. If you did not do that, recall your best experience of conflict now. Do the insights of this chapter give you further understanding about what made it a good experience?

3. When you are in a conflict, which, if either, of empowerment or recognition comes easiest to you? Have you ever experienced both of these in the same conflict? If so would you tell the group about it?

4. In the closing paragraphs, I speak of my experience of the spiritual dimension of conflict transformation. Have you ever experienced a conflict and its resolution as a spiritual experience? In what ways?

5. Are there ways you have discovered conflicts to be redemptive or transforming? A spiritual experience? In what ways?

3

Overcoming the Barriers to Creative Conflict

... I am aware, sisters and brothers, that these promises often have a hollow ring, for many of us have experienced anger and conflict so differently from that. There are wounds on our bodies and souls from past conflicts. We have also received well-intentioned but wrong interpretations of the Bible's teachings on conflict. And, we may have formed bad habits as regards anger and conflict. However, it need not stay that way. Ours is a gospel that invites us to begin again and is imbued with the power to change us ...

FOR YOUR PERSONAL OR GROUP WORSHIP

Scripture

Welcome those who are weak in faith, but not for the purpose of quarreling over opinions. (Romans 14:1)

Live in harmony with one another; do not be haughty, but associate with the lowly; do not claim to be wiser than you are. Do not repay anyone evil for evil, but take thought for what is noble in the sight of all. If it is possible, so far as it depends on you, live peaceably with all. (Romans 12:16–18)

A Word to Ponder

You've got self-righteous people on all sides arguing with other self-righteous people. God is saying No to ... these little debates we're having in the church while hundreds of thousands of people are starving to death. (Theologian Shirley Guthrie on the repeated debates in the Presbyterian Church (U.S.A.) on homosexuality.)[1]

---

1. "Voices of 2001," *The Christian Century*, December 19–26, 2001, 6.

Addressing conflict is part of the work of the church. . . . What matters is how we deal with one another. Our goal is not the absence of conflict, but a common purpose and a deep commitment to God and to one another as a church family. (Mary Day Miller)[2]

FOR YOUR THOUGHT AND REFLECTION

We have spoken both of the possible gifts and of the redemptive possibilities in anger-conflict. While we may be ready to admit that possibility, too often those good experiences are far from us. When we have sensed a conflict coming, it has not felt like good news. Rather, our feelings have been tension, dread, and looking for a way to escape it.

And when we have had the conflict, too often we do not feel good about it as an aftertaste. More often, we often feel like the respected church elder of whom Larry A. Dunn speaks. This gifted leader sat with head in hands, quietly sobbing. He asked, "What have I become? This conflict has made me someone I'm not proud of."[3] His cry is echoed by many of us. At some time, conflict has made us, both individuals and churches, something we are not proud of. How deeply we need to learn to be the same people when in conflict that we are at other times, and how good it will be if we can claim the same grace in conflict that we do in other parts of our life together. There are many barriers that make dealing with conflict all the more difficult.

Perhaps if we name, identify, and reflect on these barriers, they will lose some of their power over us. It may be that then we will find strategies to reduce their impact on us. In this chapter, I will name as many of those barriers that I have found and begin to consider how they may be dealt with.

Barrier—Early Experiences and Lessons in Home and Church

For those of us raised in active church homes, the first two barriers may be closely intertwined. *One is the first lesson (or lessons) learned about conflict in our families of origin*—either explicit or implicit, spoken or unspoken, what we experienced or what we did not. *The second may be*

---

2. Mary Day Miller, "Facing Conflict in the Small Church," 16.
3. Larry A. Dunn, "Transforming Identity in Conflict," 38.

what we experienced or were taught at our churches, perhaps in Sunday or Bible School.

Think for a moment about your earliest experiences of conflict in the family where you first belonged. Was there shouting and screaming? Did it frighten you? Was there no visible conflict at all between your parents? If you had siblings, was there competition? How was it handled? How were you advised concerning bullies or other conflicts in the neighborhood and school?

Think also about what you experienced or learned at church. Can you remember the first Christian message you received about conflict? What was it? The vast majority of people I ask remember that first message as "Good little Christian girls and boys don't...."

I cannot remember the first lessons I was taught at church about anger, but I can vividly still feel the impact of those teachings on me. Somehow, by age nine, I believed that if someone was angry with you when you died, you wouldn't go to heaven. Try as I might, I cannot call up what I was told that led me to believe this. I suspect it was some well meaning but misinformed lesson on Matthew 5:22. "... I say to you that if you are angry with a brother or sister, you will be liable to judgment; and if you insult a brother or sister, you will be liable to the council; and if you say 'You fool,' you will be liable to the hell of fire." Either it was a misinformed lesson on that text or my misunderstanding of that lesson or verse that led to my faulty belief. (We will examine that verse directly in the next chapter.)

However you read it, that verse does not say if someone is angry with you, you cannot go to heaven. But I believed that. And then my father died! He was a good rural pastor but also sometimes a stern disciplinarian. In "released time" religious education from public school, he had come down hard on some mischievous boys. I trembled in fear that they were still angry and prevented my father's admission to heaven! No one knew of this fear hidden within me, nor did they know of my great relief when Donald, one of those boys, spoke to me. "My parents said I couldn't go to your dad's funeral. But he meant so much to me that I snuck away and went to the funeral in my overalls." What a relief!

By age nine, it was ground into my nervous system that anger was powerful enough to keep someone else or me from God's presence! Another person's anger at that! No wonder that I have had problems with discovering how to express my anger. I have had lessons to learn and things to unlearn about anger and conflict.

But I am not alone in this. A friend told me that family-faith communicated a different message to her that also kept her from expressing anger and conflict. From early childhood on, she was taught, "Joy stands for *Jesus, Others, You.* Jesus first, others second, you last." Always last, far last. She said she hoped that someone would be coming behind her also putting Jesus first and others (her included) second. But that caring provision for her didn't seem to happen. Still, she strongly believed it was not right to engage in conflict for her rights and needs. Not until years later did she read anew "You shall love your neighbor as yourself," and realize that there was love for self as well as love for neighbor in that command. Therefore, loving, caring, and providing for oneself is fitting, as is anger and conflict about violation of those legitimate needs. She feels much healthier now with wholesome conflict as a part of her lifestyle. But out of her childlike interpretation of a widespread Christian teaching, it has been a long hard struggle to get there.

Yet another friend recalls her father telling her sister and her over and over again, "Smithtons don't get mad." She never heard a raised voice in her home, never saw her parents negotiate a difference. This largely wholesome and deeply devout home left her, however, without a clear understanding and freedom to deal with the inevitable conflicts and pains of life.

While the father in this particular family applied his teaching to himself as well as to his wife and daughters, this widespread teaching is more frequently applied to females. Traditionally, boys and girls have been taught differently about anger. Often girls are especially taught to suppress anger and aggression. They are to be good caretakers and keep the peace. It is emphasized that nice girls don't get angry. This teaching does not serve them well, for it means that many girls do not learn the confrontational skills they will need if faced with abuse, which is so widespread today.[4] Good assertive strategies are helpful in lesser conflicts and crises as well.

Well-intentioned but misinformed (or misunderstood) influences in early childhood do complicate our doing conflict in a free and redemptive way. And, we might add, our confusion and pain continues when, as

---

4. Carroll Saucy, *The Gift of Anger*, 22.

adults, we do not reexamine these beliefs, reformulate our assumptions, or learn skills commensurate with a more mature understanding.

For a long time, I have been deeply upset that my childhood church misled me so badly on this subject of anger and conflict. However, my more recent studies inform me that this has been the dominant church teaching for centuries. Andrew Lester speaks of the "anger-is-sin" tradition. This tradition begins with selection of particular Bible verses over others. It continues with the writings of early church leaders. In the fourth and fifth centuries, John Cassian, a monk, desert father, and founder of monasteries, wrote convincingly that anger is the most powerful of the passions. He called anger a "pernicious vice," one that damages our life with God, endangers our immortal souls, and keeps us from the wisdom and righteousness of God. The sixth century Pope, Gregory the Great, accepted much of Cassian's teaching and listed anger among the primary or capital sins. This resulted in the idea of deadly sins. By the Middle Ages, anger was firmly entrenched as one of the Seven Deadly Sins.[5] In spite of much insightful scientific study and gradually changing attitudes about anger, the view of anger-as-sin is deeply embedded in both individual and church psyches and has wreaked much havoc in both places.

Barrier—Long Standing Bad Habits

If those are the first two barriers, there are more. Third, out of this *we have long-standing bad habits for dealing with conflict among us.* These bad habits may be personal, but they may also be habits of a family, a church, a community, or an institution. Recently I heard tell of a Baptist deacon who was shipwrecked and marooned on an island all by himself, for years. When help came, his rescuers noted that he had built three huts, and they asked him what the three were. He responded, "The first is my home, and the second is my church." "The third one?" "That's my former church."

This tongue-in-cheek tale picks on my denomination, the Baptists, pointing to our tendency to the primitive reactions of fight or flight whenever conflict comes. It also implies that any one of us cannot even get along with oneself! Power plays, name calling, manipulations, splits, blowups—these can become far too common and taken for granted in church life. Too often it is assumed that to eliminate conflict, we must

---

5. Andrew Lester, *The Angry Christian: A Theology for Care and Counseling,* 125–27.

eliminate those with whom we disagree—fire the minister, or freeze out the opponents, or leave the church. The church in the story of three men and a calf (that I related in the introduction) had hardened into "north of town" and "south of town" groups and fully expected that some irritating conflict would come along every now and then. Only new Christians sensed there was something radically wrong with that picture and did not want to be part of it.

Of course, the New Testament makes clear that church conflict is as old as the first band of disciples gathered by Jesus. Conflict will always be with us. My point of view is that it *should* always be with us. The test is *how* we conflict with each other.

There are bad habits to be overcome if we are to conflict as the loving, respectful family of God.

Barriers—Incivility and Polarization

Yet another barrier is that our *society is becoming increasingly uncivil.* There is lack of respect (and certainly no reverence) for the individuals and groups on the other side of any issue.

We see this lack of civility in the political realm. Dirty tricks, name calling, sweeping assumptions, innuendo, intentional planting of untrue rumors—all this and more takes place in political contests.

We see incivility in the marketplace as well. Do anything, say anything, promise anything, pretend great care and compassion for the person with whom you speak—so long as it helps you make the sale. Further, persons who make foolish investments "should have their heads handed to them on a platter."

We see incivility in sports. The language speaks of "killing," "annihilating," or "crushing" an opponent. One player is fondly nicknamed "the assassin" because of the large number of opponents he injures.

We use similar language in describing public discourse. An able debater is said to have "destroyed" the argument of an opponent. An argument "goes up in flames." Legislators "kill" bills.[6]

Parents sometimes worry about the impact of the violence in media—TV, movies, rap and other popular music—hardly noticing that there is just as much violence in public discourse. And, all too frequently,

---

6. A thoughtful discussion of the erosion and needed re-growth of civility is found in Stephen L. Carter. *Civility: Manners, Morals, and the Etiquette of Democracy.*

there is violence in the way family members speak to each other and treat each other as well.

A barrier to constructive conflict is our being affected by the uncivil attitude and language of our culture and allowing it to invade our churches and homes.

Yet another barrier is the increased *polarization* of society and church. When we polarize, we absolutize our position and the people who agree with us. We tend to demonize the people and viewpoints that oppose us. People can become so committed, so engrossed in a cause or issue that it becomes the obsession of their lives. Any who stand in opposition deserve whatever attacks they get. Constitutional scholar Charles Haynes has noted, "The public square in America is a very angry place ... [this] doesn't bode well for the U.S."[7]

Not only the public square but also the Christian Church has become a very angry place. And this does not bode well for the church. Polarized against Christian brothers and sisters on sensitive issues of our day, we too often engage in a sort of verbal and tactical "holy war" against them. Our passionate commitment to our issue may blind us to the gospel truth that our opponent is also a person in God's image, one for whom Christ died, a member of the church which Jesus loved, and for which he gave his life.

Ethicist Edward Stevens describes the current climate in this way—

> So the big weapons are firing. The war goes on. Each side, secure in its self-limited and self-righteous vision, has contempt for the other. There is no dialogue, no conversation, no listening to the enemy.... The tactics of intimidation bring an end to dialogue. People of good will are divided from each other and silenced. [This way of conflict] destroys love, destroys compassion, destroys community. That is its biggest sin.[8]

Charles Simeon, reflecting on a theological conflict of his day in the nineteenth century, wrote, "The truth is not in the middle, not in one extreme, but in both extremes."[9] Simeon was pointing to the Christian concept of paradox, the view that truth may be found in two seemingly

---

7. Quoted in Robert Wuthnow, *Christianity and Civil Society*, 53.

8. Edward Stevens, *Developing Moral Imagination: Case Studies in Practical Morality*, 138.

9. J. LeBron McBride, *Spiritual Crisis: Surviving Trauma to the Soul*, 83.

contradictory positions, beliefs, or arguments. That concept of paradox and the invitation to dialogue—your truth and my truth might lead to bigger, vaster truth—have been missing from much of the conversation among disagreeing Christian people of late. True, talking and thinking about paradox is extremely hard work. Too often, we take the easy but destructive way out—sweeping statements, attacks, and name-calling.

Our all too deep-seated polarization from each other is standing in the way of our constructive conflict.

Barriers—Pride and Confusion

There are still more aspects to this problem. John Paul Lederach tells of coming to a church to help it deal with some dilemmas that had led to conflict. During the first meeting, one young man did not speak at all. However, after all the others left, he went up to John and told him, "You know, the real problem is that some people here are not right with the Lord. If they got right with the Lord, things would clear up here."[10] There is probably a partial truth in the young man's statement. But there is also blindness. His assumption seemed to be, "I am right with God, and you are not." And that is why there is discord.

Of course, at times we may have good reason to think we have discovered God's will on an issue, and that others are wrong. Still that does not give us permission to attack or dismiss some of God's people, who *might* be wrong on this issue.

Conflict is not a sin; it may be a necessary part of searching for God's leadership and guidance. Our bogging down in conflict, our wounding of those with whom we disagree, our narrowness in our own vision so that we cannot see another's point of view, that is sin. But it is sin that is part of all of us.

Still another barrier to redemptive conflict is our individual and collective spiritual pride.

William Willimon points to yet another barrier, "*One fundamental reason why congregations are plagued by conflict is that there is no consensus within the congregation about the purpose and nature of the church.*"[11]

Willimon is speaking of the local congregation, where, due to the increased mobility of today's society, there is rapid turnover and little

---

10. John Paul Lederach, *The Journey Toward Reconciliation*, 100.

11. William Willimon, *Preaching About Conflict in the Local Church*, 27. The italics are added.

continuity of membership in some churches. There is also other widespread mobility—from one denomination to another, for example, or from religious indifference to religious involvement. No longer are our church groups firmly founded upon well known and agreed upon Christian teachings. This lack of a shared biblical-theological foundation contributes to confusion in people's concepts of what a church is and why it exists.

Beyond that, "What is the church, and what is its mission?" is a key and basic question that needs to be reconsidered in each generation. It deserves prayerful and searching study of scriptures and more. From the cries of the hurting world, we are called to grow and change.

And so, not only is our confusion about the church and its mission a reason for our conflict. Our confusion about church and mission should be the very first topic on which we carry on constructive conflict. (We will begin this task in chapter six.)

In fairness to us all, let us acknowledge that our conflicts are often over cherished values and beliefs. These values and beliefs are so much a part of us, that hearing and discussing them with others, much less critiquing and debating, is extremely difficult. (We will speak more of value conflicts in chapter eight.) And yet, we are called to do our best, respectfully, humbly. For, we are God's people. The vitality of our witness depends on it.

Response—Perspective Through Laughing At Ourselves

If those are at least most of the barriers, how do we overcome them? We might start with John Paul Lederach's perspective. He ponders why his denomination, the Mennonites, who do so much good in peace-making in various trouble spots of the world, do so poorly with each other in conflicts in their own churches. As he ponders this, he offers a playful-serious "Unspoken Ten Commandments of Conflict in the Mennonite Church." As you read them over, you may agree with me that these apply to many other churches, yours and mine included, as well.

1. Thou shalt be nice. Always be nice. Yea, I say unto thee, "niceness" is the essence of Christianity.

2. Thou shalt not confront each other in public. Confrontation is nasty and unmanageable. If ever in doubt about confrontation, refer to commandment number 1.

3. Should thou ever have the distasteful experience of confrontation, thou shalt not listen to thine enemy, but shalt prepare thy defense while the enemy is still speaking. Yea, I say unto thee, listening raises questions that weaken thy defense and may lead to compromise, impurity, and, heaven forbid, self-reflection. It is dangerous to change thy mind or admit that thou wert wrong. Truth is unchangeable.

4. Speak not with contentious folks who disagree with thee or who have raised thy "righteous anger." Thou shalt seek out and talk to others about them. Yea, more, dear brothers and sisters, speak only with nice people who agree with thee. By speaking only with those with whom thou dost agree, thou wilt experience the true support of community.

5. Remember that thou art of noble and decent character, even a pacifist, and thou shalt not show thine emotions in public.

6. Men, be rational. Do not show weakness through emotions like crying or anger. It is better for thee to disengage from a situation of conflict and remain silent than to show uncontrolled emotion.

7. Women, thou shalt not defend thyself vigorously, nor "nag" incessantly, or they may call thee the dreadful *B* word. Thou shalt be prepared to have thine opinions ignored, realizing that those same opinions may be accepted as valid if later stated by a man. Thou shalt not gripe about this in the presence of men.

8. If thou dost not like the way things are going in the church, thou shalt blame the pastor. Most problems can be traced to the pastor. If the pastor is a saint, then blame the church council. If the church council is clean, then blame "them." Keep it a generic an undefined "they" or "some people I know." If thou cannot find anyone to blame, leave the church Verily, I say, a church where there is nobody to blame is not worth staying in.

9. If thou must confront, save thine energy, frustration, and irritation for the annual budget meeting. God gave annual budget meetings to bring congregational catharsis.

10. Dear Christian sisters and brothers, in a holy nutshell I say unto ye all, thou shalt not have conflict in the church.

> Conflict is a sign of sin. Yea, should conflict emerge, pray that God may convict and convert thine erring enemies.[12]

Our smiles, chuckles, and laughter at ourselves may the first stage of our healing. With our laughter, may we begin to believe that none of these barriers need overcome our desire to be the reconciled body of Christ. We can learn and grow and become the stronger for it.

Response—Self-Examination and Reconsideration

We continue by hearing anew Romans 12:2: "Do not be conformed to this world, but be transformed by the renewing of your minds, so that you may discern what is the will of God—what is good and acceptable and perfect." The new hearing of this verse might be a call to reexamine our anger and conflict style with each other. Too much of our recent conflict has resembled "the world"—the incivility, the polarity, the disregard for others. We are called to invite God to transform our conflicts.

In this connection, William Willimon gives us food for thought:

> Because the church is rightly judged by the character of the people who comprise the church, our response to conflict is part of our witness to the world that Jesus Christ makes it possible to live with one another in hope and peace. Christ has given us the means of living with one another without the fear and violence that constitute human relations in the world.[13]

After we have gained some self-perspective from laughter and committed our dealings with each other to God's transformation, what next? We commit ourselves to an ethic of anger and conflict. That is; we choose to seek responsible living with anger-conflict.

I strongly believe that we need to disavow the "anger-is-sin" point of view. At the same time we need also to challenge and reject the "anger-is-lord" point of view. That is, the widespread belief that our emotions rule us and we are helplessly co-opted by them. We express this mistaken view when we say we are swept away by our passions, or that our anger overcame us, or carried us away, or blinded us, so that we couldn't help ourselves. This is what Lester calls the "myth of passivity."[14]

---

12. Lederach, op. cit., 101–3.
13. Willimon, op. cit., 44.
14. Lester, op. cit., 62–63.

We are ethically responsible to explore what has shaped our emotions. We are equally responsible for how our emotions, including anger and conflict are expressed. Personal and group responsibility and ethical commitment are foundational in our overcoming our present impasses. The rest of the book will flesh out this basic response.

We have work to do! Let's proceed by next directing our conversation to the Bible. We will look for stories of and teachings about conflict and reconciliation. Also, we will direct our search for priorities on the nature and purpose of the church. We will further need to explore how to talk with each other across our varying ways of interpreting scripture. For now, smile, have hope, and commit to the journey.

QUESTIONS AND ACTIVITIES FOR GROUP REFLECTION

1. List the various barriers to creative conflict that I mention. What barriers did I fail to mention? Which of these are most troubling to you personally?

2. What do you recall about your earliest childhood experience and learning about anger-conflict, either at home or at church? In what ways are those teachings still a part of you? Does this teaching from your childhood feel comfortable, or are there parts of that teaching you'd like to leave behind? How do adults relearn and rethink childish beliefs?

3. Do you recognize any bad habits that have crept into your way of working on conflict? If so, what are they? How do we break habits such as these?

4. What, if any, loss of civility in our society concerns you most? What are your suggestions for bringing more civility back to church discourse?

5. What was your response to Lederach's "Unspoken Ten Commandments"? Did they make you laugh? If so, at which ones did you laugh the most? Would you like to venture a guess why?

6. As thoughtful Christian adults, how can we overcome barriers to effective dialogue on controversial issues? What would you add to the beginning steps suggested at the end of this chapter?

PART TWO

Revisiting the Bible for Perspectives on Conflict

4

Anger, Conflict, and Reconciliation in the Bible

. . . And so, let us turn to our Bible to hear the gospel of peace and peace-making that is found there. Though there is much conflict and struggle recorded in our scripture, we will also discover heart-warming stories of reconciliation within families, between brothers and sisters, in churches, and among tribes and nations. We will also find inspired prophetic visions of peace beyond anything the world has yet known.

The gospels describe our Lord addressing conflicts among his followers and seeking reconciliation and understanding even with his fiercest critics. The latter parts of the New Testament portray a church at work to heal its divisions so that the gospel might be clearly experienced. Most basically, the Bible points to God in Christ as our peace, the Source who unites us all . . .

FOR YOUR PERSONAL OR GROUP WORSHIP

Scripture

". . . truly to see your face is like seeing the face of God." (Genesis 33:10—Jacob to brother Esau after a strong conflict and an absence of twenty years)

"Steadfast love and faithfulness will meet;
    righteousness and peace will kiss each other." (Ps 85:10)

"I urge Euodia and I urge Syntyche to be of the same mind in the Lord. Yes, and I ask you also, my loyal companion to help these women, for they have struggled beside me in the work of the gospel . . . whose names are in the book of life." (Phil 4:2–3)

A Word to Ponder

> The reconciliation between humanity and God has an immediate and intimate horizontal impact. Humans who were alienated to each other are now reconciled in Christ, at least theologically. . . . Because we are reconciled to God through the cross, all of us from whatever human identity group are brought into a new oneness. . . . The challenge to the early church was how to live out that theological reality of reconciliation and oneness amidst the personal and social baggage of the old order." (Daniel Buttry)[1]

FOR YOUR THOUGHT AND REFLECTION

The focus of our conversation now shifts from anger and conflict in our present experience to that of those in our heritage of faith. In this chapter we will do an overview of stories and teachings about anger and conflict in the Bible. In the next chapter, we will explore ways to dialogue about our different ways of interpreting the Bible. And in the following one, we will listen to the Bible for the highest priorities God has for God's people in this century and beyond.

We will not lack for biblical material to explore. It is estimated that there are from four to five hundred references to human or divine anger in the scriptures! Of all these, my focus is on divine guidance for understanding and managing our anger and conflicts.

A beginning point for our discussion is to be reminded that the Bible (both Hebrew Bible and New Testament) portrays a passionate God who longs for fellowship and obedience from God's creatures and who is often disappointed and angry when this is not so. Indeed, when exploring this topic, Carroll Saussy noted a multitude of references to God's anger throughout scripture and felt a necessity to find a fitting interpretation of divine anger-wrath as part of her constructing a theology of anger. She considered five possible competing interpretations: 1. The Biblical God is an abuser; 2. God's anger is in tension with God's love; 3. God's wrath is a way of punishing God's people for their disobedience; 4. The Biblical account of a wrathful God is a human attempt to find meaning in the midst of chaos and loss; 5. God's wrath is a projection of humankind's wrath.

---

1. Daniel L. Buttry, *Christian Peacemaking: From Heritage to Hope*, 29–30.

Saussy arrived at her own interpretation: 6. God's anger is a mystery beyond rational explanation. She noted that human beings are not privy to God's inner life. This author understands God as having a great vision for the human family—and great frustration when, time and again, these very humans do not live out that vision![2] Within that understanding of God's anger, there is certainly room for free exploration and discussion of the topic of anger itself.

At times it may seem to us that God's anger is excessive. For example in 2 Samuel 24, God incites David to take a census in violation of law and then punishes with pestilence so that seventy thousand people died. In Numbers 16, God's anger at a rebellious people is such that the whole congregation will be consumed. By quick action of an atoning sacrifice, "only" fourteen thousand, seven hundred are killed. The interpretation of such anger passages is shrouded in mystery.

At the same time, the Bible also teaches that God has an ultimate purpose for humankind and creation—that we be reconciled to each other and to God. In scripture we find divine passion, love, frustration, and sometimes anger, all in the goal of a greater harmony than we have yet known. That, in some mysterious combination, was what Saussy discerned for her theology of anger. It can also serve as a starting place for us in this exploration. It offers a possible overarching view of the stories and guidance about the anger, conflict, and reconciliation we find in the Bible. We will explore these experiences in a variety of settings.[3]

The Hebrew Bible

Conflict-Reconciliation in Families

Early in the Bible, in two succeeding generations, stories are told of conflict and reconciliation in families. The first is about Isaac and Rebekah and their sons, Esau and Jacob (Gen 25–33. All chapter references in this section are from Genesis). Conflict starts early—when Rebecca is pregnant with twins, "The children struggled together within her" (25:22). It continues—in the birth canal, the second born is fighting for the favored

---

2. Carroll Saussy, *The Gift of Anger*, 67–80.

3. In the summary that follows, I acknowledge how much I learned from "A Bible Study Manual on Conflict Transformation" by Daniel L. Buttry, and self-published by the author.

firstborn family position. He is born pulling at the heel of his slightly older brother. Fittingly, they name him "Jacob" which means grasper.

This battle goes on, made all the worse by parental favoritism. "When the boys grew up, Esau was a skillful hunter, a man of the field, while Jacob was a quiet man, living in tents. Isaac loved Esau, because he was fond of game; but Rebekah loved Jacob" (25:27–28).

The younger Jacob bargains Esau's birthright (that included the largest share of the inheritance) for a bowl of food served to the famished but short sighted Esau. Then, Jacob tricks his aged father into giving him his brother's family blessing as well (25:29–34; 27:1–40). Enraged, Esau plots, "'The days of mourning for my father are approaching; then I will kill my brother Jacob'" (27:41).

Rebekah again conspires on behalf of her favorite son. She persuades Isaac to send him away to find a wife among her kinfolk, far away. That journey and sojourn is quite a story in itself. It includes conniving, cheating, tricking—and two life shaking encounters with almighty God (28–31).

Twenty years later, Jacob decides to return home, which means he must face Esau. He learns that Esau is approaching with 400 men! Jacob sends gifts and splits his family into two groups in the hope that some will survive. Then Jacob goes to meet his brother.

As they approach each other after all these years, how will the wronged brother respond? ". . . Esau ran to meet him, and embraced him and fell on his neck and kissed him, and they wept" (33:4). At first, Esau refuses Jacob's many gifts, but Jacob pleads that he accept them "for truly to see your face is like seeing the face of God—since you have received me with such favor" (33:10).

Jacob, however, does not travel alongside Esau, nor settle right next to him. That could have led to new competition and conflict. At the end of this story, two formerly estranged brothers are reconciled, though keeping a safe and respectable distance from each other.

Still another family conflict story comes in the very next generation. Some families are slow learners! Jacob—now named Israel—also has a favorite son, Joseph, child of his favorite wife, child of his old age.

Both father and favorite son seem oblivious to what they are doing to the rest of the family. Israel buys Joseph a very special robe that sets him apart from the others. Further, Joseph snitches on his brothers and gives a bad report on them to his father. Further still, when he has grandiose dreams of their grain sheaves bowing to his, and then even the sun, moon, and eleven stars bowing down to him, he has the insensitivity to tell them all about it.

Not surprisingly, they don't like him very much! When they come upon him at a safe distance from father, they seize him, throw him into a pit and intend to kill him. Only a passing caravan (and perhaps one brother's softening a bit) stir a better plan—sell him into slavery into Egypt and *say* he is dead (37).

Joseph is sold to an Egyptian official, Potiphar, who sees that God prospers what Joseph attempts and so makes him an overseer. But he is falsely accused of seducing Potiphar's wife and is thrown in prison. In prison, Joseph correctly interprets the dreams of two other prisoners.

After two more years in prison, Pharaoh has a dream no one can interpret and the servant cupbearer remembers him. Joseph is brought to Pharaoh and interprets the dream—of seven sleek, fat cows eaten by seven thin, ugly ones. Joseph tells Pharaoh that there will be seven years of great plenty throughout the land followed by seven years of famine. During the years of plenty, food should be collected and stored to survive the famine. The interpretation and the dream seemed so wise to Pharaoh that he puts Joseph second in authority in the entire kingdom to carry out the plan (39–41).

After the seven years of plenty, the famine does indeed come all over that region. And so in time, ten of Joseph's brothers come to Egypt, requesting to buy food. They do not recognize the Egyptian official as their brother, but true to his dream, they all bow down before him (42:6).

Again, it is now at least twenty years since Joseph has seen his brothers. Joseph puts his brothers through a series of tests to see if they have really changed—detaining one brother, insisting that they bring their younger brother, putting they money they paid back in their sacks, putting his royal drinking cup in youngest brother Benjamin's bag and threatening to detain him (42–44).

When they plead eloquently to let Benjamin go free, and when brother Judah offers himself in place, Joseph can see the change. "And he wept so loudly that the Egyptians heard it" (45:2). He reveals who he is and tells his dismayed siblings, "Do not be distressed, or angry with yourselves, because you sold me here; for God sent me before you to preserve life" (45:5). He ordered they bring their father and all their households to Egypt to be cared for, which they did (46–50).

After their father's death, Joseph's brothers are again fearful. And so again they approach Joseph begging for forgiveness. He weeps as he speaks to them, "Do not be afraid. Am I in the place of God? Even though you intended to do harm to me, God intended it for good ... So have no fear; I myself will provide for you and your little ones" (50:19–21).

Conflict-Reconciliation Among the Tribes and Nations

In the midst of many accounts of frequent wars, some of them involving revenge and annihilation of foes, there are occasional accounts of reconciliation and peacemaking. Here are two of those stories.

In Joshua 22:10–34, there is an inter-tribal conflict within the new nation. When the children of Israel came to the territory where they would settle under Joshua's leadership, nine and a half of the tribes settled west of the Jordan, and two and a half tribes settled east of the Jordan.

The easterners decide to build an altar "of great size" near the Jordan River. When the westerners hear this, they assemble and are prepared to make war on their easterner fellow tribes folk. Before they start war, however, they wisely send a delegation of a priest's son and a chief from each of the nine west tribes to the folks in the east.

When the western delegation arrives, they do not mince words. They accuse them of "treachery" and "rebellion." They state their fears, that these easterners are contaminating the whole nation with the worship of false gods. Such actions had brought great pain in the past, and they do not want it repeated!

The easterners respond that their motives had not been understood at all. For one thing, they had no intent of offering burnt sacrifices or any other offerings. The altar was built as a witness to their children, so that they would not forget God's great guidance and blessing if the past. It was intended simply as a "copy of the altar of the Lord" (22:28).

In reflecting on this story, Joseph Sizoo commented, "Perhaps the most pressing need of the world on a human level is for strong [people] to sit face to face and speak frankly of their suspicions and fears to each other."[4] With these two delegations, this process worked, to rich results.

The westerners listen with open minds to the easterners' explanation of their actions. The leader, Phinehas, accepts what was said and compliments them on stating their stance so clearly and thus avoiding

---

4. Joseph Sizoo, "Exposition of Joshua," 660.

war. With all satisfied, the altar is named "Witness" to stand as a testimony to all that "Yahweh is God."[5]

There is an equally striking story from a time of international conflict in 2 Kings 6:8–23. The Arameans (Syrians) were making a series of raids on their southern neighbors the nation of Israel. However, these often provide unsuccessful because the Israelites seemed to know their actions before they happened. The Aramean king suspected spying within his house. However, he was told the reporting was the work of the powerful prophet of Israel, Elisha, who "tells the king of Israel what you say in your bedchamber" (6:12).

The Syrian king learns Elisha's location and sends a great army there to seize him. When Elisha's servant sees them coming, he is filled with terror until Elisha opens the servant's eyes to see all the divine protection surrounding them. Elisha prays, "Strike this people, please with blindness." It is so, and Elisha speaks to the blinded soldiers promising to take them to the man they seek. Helpless, perhaps with each soldier putting a hand on the shoulder of the one in front, the one in very front with his hand on Elisha, the army is led into the walled capital city Samaria, into the hands of their enemies!

When the King of Israel sees this strange turn of events, he asks Elisha, "Father, should I kill them?" (6:21). Elisha responds that he should feed them instead. "So he prepares for them a great feast. After they ate and drank, he sends them on their way, and they go to their master." In response to this unexpected mercy and kindness, the story concludes, "And the Arameans no longer came raiding into the land of Israel" (6:23).

As delightful as this story is, it must be noted that the ceasing of hostilities and raiding was temporary. The next story in 2 Kings says that "Some time later" the Aramean king again attacked Samaria.

One of these stories describes a very small intertribal conflict that was resolved, and the other describes an act of mercy that temporarily halted hostilities and raids between two countries. Though small incidents, they are signs of hope. Indeed, they are expressions of a deep hunger for a lasting peace among all of God's people.

---

5. Buttry, *Christian Peacemaking*, 34–35.

The Vision of Shalom

The concept of peace—shalom—is a deep and abiding vision in the Bible. Shalom is a comprehensive word that includes many things. Among these are wholeness, well being, prosperity untouched by violence or misfortune, and the free growth of the person. But above all it means harmonious community with others as the foundation of life.[6]

The Psalmists speak often of such peace-shalom. Here are a few brief examples:

- A plaintive cry, "Too long have I had my dwelling among those who hate peace. I am for peace; but when I speak, they are for war" (Ps 120:6–7).

- A call to prayer for the city, "Pray for the peace of Jerusalem: 'May they prosper who love you. Peace be within your walls, and security within your towers.' For the sake of my relatives and friends I will say, 'Peace be within you'" (Ps 122:6–8).

- A prayer for the restoration of God's favor, "Let me hear what God the Lord will speak, for he will speak peace to his people. . . . Steadfast love and faithfulness will meet; righteousness and peace will kiss each other" (Ps 85:8, 10).

. . . and these are only the briefest of examples of the frequent theme of hope for peace among God's people and in the world.

The prophets joined their voices. Both Micah and Isaiah spoke of a profound future:

> He [God] shall judge between many peoples,
>   and shall arbitrate between strong nations far away
> they shall beat their swords into plowshares
>   and their spears into pruning hooks
> nation shall not lift up sword against nation,
>   neither shall they learn war any more;
> but they shall all sit under their own vines and under their own fig trees,
>   and no one shall make them afraid;
> for the mouth of the Lord has spoken
> (Mic. 4:3–4; see also Isa. 2:1–4).

---

6. C. F. Evans, "Peace" in Alan Richardson, *A Theological Wordbook of the Bible*, 165.

Wise Anger

Before completing our survey of anger-conflict in Hebrew scripture, there are two more themes to explore. One of these is the treatment of anger in wisdom literature.

The wisdom books, Proverbs in particular, and also Ecclesiastes contain many statements about anger. Here are some of them from Proverbs: "One who is quick-tempered acts foolishly" (14:17). "Whoever is slow to anger has great understanding, but one who has a hasty temper exalts folly" (14:29). "Those who are hot-tempered stir up strife, but those who are slow to anger calm contention" (15:18). "One who is slow to anger is better than the mighty, and one whose temper is controlled than one who captures a city" (16:32). "Wrath is cruel, anger is overwhelming, but who is able to stand before jealousy?" (27:4). "Those with good sense are slow to anger, and it is their glory to overlook an offense" (19:11). Here is one from Ecclesiastes: "Do not be quick to anger, for anger lodges in the bosom of fools" (7:9).

Some have interpreted these verses to say that good people are those who never experience or express anger. A more discerning reading of these and kindred verses leads to a different conclusion, however. Rather, these verses teach us how to be wise with our anger. As Andrew Lester notes, the verses do not caution against anger itself, but against temper tantrums, explosive hostility, and immature hot tempers. What this scripture does do is "challenge us to be careful with our anger and to take responsibility for evaluating when to get angry, what to get angry at, and how to express the anger."[7]

Anger at God

The other theme to consider is this—is it permissible to not only be angry with God but to express that anger?

The answer given in a number of Psalms is: "Yes, of course!" If God is a faithful covenant giver, and if God does not seem to be keeping the promises made, this can be challenged with all the anger and force appropriate to the occasion. Phrases from Psalm 44 provide a prime example: "You have rejected and abased us.... You have made us like sheep for slaughter, and have scattered us among the nations. You have sold

---

7. Lester, *The Angry Christian*, 140–41.

your people for a trifle... You have made us the taunt of our neighbors. ... You have broken us."

When God is experienced as abandoning relationships, trivializing deep human concerns, and/or deceiving people, the psalmists' anger flows freely! Sometimes the one who expresses the anger finds relief from the expression of it, sometimes not. At times, there is promise that fortunes will be restored in the future but not always. Sometimes there is calmness and resolution at the conclusion of such psalms, sometimes not. That such passages are in our scripture is important for our understanding of anger and conflict. As Lester notes, "Expressing anger toward God may indeed be an act of honesty that restores authentic relationship with the divine."[8]

The New Testament

We turn now to Christian scriptures. Our survey moves on to explore conflict and reconciliation in the gospels. We look to Jesus as our guide and empowering person as we live with these issues. A sensitive reading of the gospels discerns a Jesus who experiences and expresses a full range of human emotions, anger among them. What we find in his life and in his teaching about how to deal with each other in conflict is important to our search.

The Disciples and Jesus

We begin by looking at Jesus' disciples. The gospels describe Jesus calling several disciples individually or in pairs. At a later time, from a larger group of followers, he chose twelve to be his disciples (students and close followers) as well as apostles (those he would send forth with his message) (Mark 3:13–19). The makeup of that group guaranteed that there would be lively dynamics among them. Two were called "sons of thunder" and one called "Peter" or rock, because of a coming, not a present characteristic. But there were other possible tensions as well. Clarence Jordan once noted that the twelve included Mathew a tax collector and Simon, quite possibly a Zealot. Zealots had made a vow to kill tax collectors. Jordan quipped, "Unless I miss my guess, Jesus had to sleep between those two boys!"

---

8. Ibid., 141.

Any newly formed community is tested by how it handles the early conflicts that will surely arise. The disciples were no exception. Not long after they had been chosen, they "argued with one another who was the greatest" (Mark 9:34) Indeed, most of their conflicts among themselves seemed to be about privilege, position, and power. In Mark, just a chapter after this first incident of competition, James and John (perhaps aided by their mother [Matt 20:20]), ask Jesus, "Grant us to sit, one at your right hand and one at your left, in your glory" (Mark 10:37). "When the ten heard it, they were angry with the two brothers" (Matt 20:24). This dispute among the twelve about who is the greatest continued even into the upper room as they ate a last meal together on the night before Jesus died (Luke 22:24).

Jesus confronted these outbursts of intra-group conflict in a variety of ways. In the first instance, he put a child in their midst and urged them all to become as children. The next time, he pointed to the high cost of discipleship—a cup to drink, a baptism with which to be baptized. He also told them that what they asked was not his to give. In the third instance, near the end of his life, he knelt before each, washed that disciple's feet, and then urged them to wash each other's feet (John 13:1–13).[9] There is great gentleness and patience in the way Jesus dealt with the competitive conflicts among his disciples.

But this does not exhaust Jesus' relationship with disciples. He was at one moment strongly affirming. When Peter recognized him as the promised one, he exclaimed, "Blessed are you. . . ." He was at the next moment equally confronting. When Peter resisted his statement that he must be killed, Jesus said, "Get behind me Satan! For you are a stumbling block to me" (Matt 16:17, 23). At times he flared at them for their lack of understanding, "Do you still not perceive or understand? Are your hearts hardened. . . . Do you not yet understand?" (Mark 8:17–21). (As we shall see, Jesus could contend with almost anything in people, except hardened hearts. To sense that hardened hearts might be a problem even of his disciples must have been painful indeed.) At other times, he was accepting and forgiving of the most grievous behavior. To Peter when predicting his denial, he said "When once you have turned back, strengthen your brothers" (Luke 22:31). He spoke to Judas when he was

---

9. This last statement is my surmise. I am combining Luke's reference to the dispute among the disciples with the gospel of John's description of Jesus' washing their feet.

about to do the betraying kiss that led to his arrest, "Friend, do what you are here to do" (Matt 26:50).

We also consider Jesus' teaching on conflict-anger. He gave a word of guidance to his wide band of disciples who would become the church as to how to deal with conflict between them. In Matt 18:15–17, he tells that if another sins against you, go and point this out when the two of you are alone; if not listened to, take along one or two witnesses and discuss it again. If that fails, bring it to the whole church. And if even that fails, "let such a one be to you as a Gentile and a tax collector" (18:17; of course, Jesus treated Gentiles and tax collectors quite well!).

The way this passage is stated, it speaks of when one has been wronged or sinned against. Many have found this equally sound guidance when there is a conflict that needs attention. Deal with it personally, one on one. If that doesn't work out, deal with it as soon as possible with the smallest number of persons appropriate to the issue. Take it to the whole church only if these steps do not succeed. But taking it to the church is preferable to letting the conflict fester for a long time.

At an earlier time, in his Sermon on the Mount (which was essentially guidance for disciples) Jesus also spoke of divine claims on us in our anger. This is a key and foundational passage that deserves our close and careful attention. In Matt 5:21–24 (the first of a series of striking new examples of how to live in this new age of God's kingdom), he gives us a command that goes beyond the old one, which was not to murder. This saying of Jesus has often confused people as to what to do with their anger just as it confused me in my childhood.

How important it is to hear what he really said, as we seek to be faithful in this important area of our lives. Beyond not murdering, he goes on, "But I say to you that if you are angry with a brother or sister, you will be liable to judgment. . . ." Is Jesus forbidding any angry feeling? Hardly. To understand this we need to give careful attention to the original Greek verb here. In particular we need to pay attention to the tense of that verb. There is a verb tense that speaks of continuing action, and that is the verb tense used here. This tells us that what he is forbidding is long term sustaining of anger, not the feeling or expression of immediate anger. A better translation than the ones we usually read would say "everyone who is continuously angry" or "everyone who keeps on being angry." The New English Bible accurately translates those words "anyone who *nurses* anger . . ." (emphasis mine). What he is telling us to leave behind is the grudge, the long term feud, that battle where no one wants a resolution. He goes on to forbid the abusive language and name calling that often go with such entrenched battles. Rather, he urges, if one is offering a gift at the altar and remembers a problem or issue with someone, first go and be reconciled, and then come, offer the gift. Rather than forbidding anger as is often assumed, Jesus' words in the Sermon on the Mount point in exactly the opposite direction. They urge a prompt, direct, and thorough dealing with the conflict and the anger.

Jesus and His World

As we look at Jesus in conflict in other areas of his life, there are two surprises. One surprise is the many relationships of trust and faith he established with people who might have been expected to be antagonists. These included:

- A Roman centurion—"I tell you, not even in Israel have I found such faith" (Luke 7:9);

- A Syro-Phoenician woman—"Woman, great is your faith!" (Matt 15:28);

- An exorcist, not his follower, expelling spirits in his name—"Do not stop him . . . . Whoever is not against us is for us" (Mark 9: 39–40);

- A Samaritan village that would not allow him to enter—When James and John wanted to call fire down on them, Jesus "turned and rebuked them. Then they went on to another village" (Luke 9:55). Also, a solitary Samaritan woman, apparently alienated from her Samaritan peers—In their conversation the woman speaks of the coming Messiah, "I am he, the one who is speaking to you" (John 4:26);

- A prostitute—". . . her sins, which were many, have been forgiven; hence she has shown great love" (Luke 7:47);

- Tax collectors and other outcasts—"Those who are well have no need of a physician, but those who are sick; I have come to call not the righteous but sinners" (Mark 2:17); and

- Indeed, the everyday people of the land responded eagerly, came in vast multitudes—He in turn had compassion on them, wanted them fed physically and spiritually and yearned for them as "sheep without a shepherd" (Mark 6:34). He lamented Jerusalem, "How often have I desired to gather your children together as a hen gathers her brood under her wings, and you were not willing!" (Luke 13:34).

The other surprise is how sharp the conflict with a group of people with whom it would seem he would have much in common. Pharisees were believers in God, heirs of the same spiritual forebears, devout in attempting to make their religion a part of their lives, students of the same Holy Scriptures as Jesus. They were the most influential religious party in the Judaism of Jesus' day, the religion of his heritage and practice.

While Jesus probably had friends among Pharisees (he did have meals in Pharisees' homes, and Pharisees did warn him of Herod's threat), there were often deep and irreconcilable differences. These conflicts appear early in the gospels, are relentless throughout, and are given vivid expression near the end of his life. As S. MacLean Gilmour noted, "The Pharisees held that both the law of Moses and the tradition of the scribes were the revelation of God's will; that the ceremonial, criminal, civil, and religious regulations of the law were all inviolable; and that the essence of obedience to the law lay in obedience to its letter."[10]

By contrast, Jesus obeyed the Torah-law-teaching but often repudiated the interpretations of the law given by the scribes. Further, he drew a distinction between the religious and ethical commands on one hand and its cultic and ceremonial regulations on the other. He saw the former as basic and permanent; the latter as peripheral and transitory. And, most basically, he called people to a new obedience in the Kingdom of God's love, an obedience that often went far beyond the claims of Torah.

These differences led to constant conflict in several areas:

- Sabbath keeping—both small (like picking a few heads of grain to eat) and large (healing longsuffering chronically ill people);
- Ceremonial washing before eating;
- Eating with people who were ceremonially unclean; and
- Fasting (or rather, not fasting).

These conflicts are constant on the pages of the gospel. Practically all of these issues are mentioned in Mark 2–3. In Mark 3:1–6, there is

---

10. Gilmour, *The Gospel Jesus Preached*, 143–44.

the only specific naming of Jesus being angry. In the synagogue on the Sabbath, he saw a man with a withered hand. He asked aloud if it were lawful to do good on the Sabbath. No one would answer him, one way or the other. "He looked around at them with anger; he was grieved at their hardness of heart, and said to the man, 'Stretch out your hand'" (3:5). Mark notes that from that early point, Pharisees and Herodians conspired to kill him.

The gospels describe Jesus as attempting to dialogue and converse with Pharisees, responding to their tests and trapping questions again and again. But this was to no avail, for the most part, as far as opening minds or un-hardening hearts. Matthew describes Jesus as giving a scathing indictment of scribes and Pharisees during the last week of his life. He calls them hypocrites, blind guides; tithers of the tiniest detail while neglecting justice mercy and faith; those who strain a gnat and swallow a camel; those who clean the outside of the plate but leave the inside filthy; and whitewashed tombs! (Matt 23).

As Jesus' ministry spread, the opposition of Pharisees was joined by temple priests and others of the privileged class known as Sadducees. Early in his ministry, Jesus showed love for the temple and tolerance of its leadership. He went there, taught there, and at least once, though he did not feel obligated to—"so that we do not give offense" (Matt 17:27)—he paid the temple tax/contribution, albeit in an unusual way.

But at the end, outraged at the abuses of temple officials, he engaged in his most physical act of anger recorded in scriptures. All of the gospels record that he drove out those who were selling in the temple, overturning the tables of money changers, and the seats of those who sold doves. (See Mark 11:15–19, for example.) John, who places this event at the beginning of Jesus' ministry, adds the detail that he made a whip of cords to drive them out (John 2:15).

Jesus stood before these folks with a new revelation about many things: who God is; what God asks of us both as to how to relate to God and how to treat each other; and what God had asked Jesus to do and be in all this. On these basic truths he could not compromise. Hardened hearts did not allow them to accept. It was a battle to the death—literally! But this did not happen until he made every effort to resolve conflict with those who resisted his message.

There were certainly other times when Jesus was angry. In Mark 10:13–14, we are told that Jesus was "indignant" (irritated, annoyed, discontented) when disciples failed to heed his teaching about the value of children and were trying to keep parents with their children from him.

There may have been other times. Was Jesus angry in the garden of Gethsemane, when he spoke to a disciple who was letting him down (and shortly would do so again), "Simon, are you asleep? Could you not keep awake one hour?" (Mark 14:37).

And was Jesus angry on the cross, angry with God in the company of the psalmists before him, when he cried out, "My God, My God, why have you forsaken me?" (Matt 27:46; Mark 15:34). We may discover more about anger-conflict-reconciliation in the life and teaching of Jesus than first we realized.

Conflict-Reconciliation in the Early Church

After the death and resurrection of Jesus, the church of his followers came into being. That first day of Pentecost after his resurrection had brought a powerful expression of the Holy Spirit's power and the attraction of thousands into faith in Christ and the Christian community. This included many Jewish people back from the dispersion throughout the known world. Many of these had adopted the universal Greek language, and, perhaps, some Greek customs. These are the folks that Luke, the author of Acts calls "Hellenists."

Among the believers in Christ were also folks who had spent their whole lives in Palestine, who spoke Aramaic, and who accepted none of the Greek customs. In Acts, these are the "Hebrews."

In Acts 6, there is recorded one of the first conflicts in this fast growing Jerusalem church. It arose out of Christian appropriation of a gracious Jewish custom—a weekly collection of money or produce to distribute among the more needy persons, particularly widows within a congregation. This early Christian community had continued this practice, but there were problems with how it was done. Possibly a subtle discrimination had crept in, and those who had always taken part didn't even notice the neglect of some of their newcomers.

At any rate, the Hellenists complained that their widows, just as deserving as Hebrew widows, were being neglected in this distribution. Is the church a community of care for all who come or not?

To the credit of the twelve apostles, there was prompt attention. With their numbers growing, proclaiming the faith and administering the needs of those in the church was more than they could handle well.

Their first responsibility was proclamation of the good news—"prayer and serving the word" (Acts 6:4).

And so they offered a solution, "Select for yourselves seven men of good standing, full of Spirit and of wisdom whom we may appoint to this task" (Acts 6:3). The decision was given to the whole community, and they picked seven from the Hellenists (as indicated by their names). The church gave the authority for this to the persons who had been discriminated against, and who, up to this point, had been powerless.

The deliberate choice to face the conflict squarely and trust in the wisdom of the community led to a most gratifying solution. Harmony was restored, and "the number of disciples increased greatly in Jerusalem, and a great many of the priests became obedient to the faith" (Acts 6:7).

As the church expanded into other places, new conflicts emerged. One conflict had to do with other new believers. The first followers of Jesus were all Jews. As the gospel spread, Gentiles, non-Jewish persons, were also convinced and became believers. But what was their status in the church? It was an issue that sooner or later the church would have to face.

It came to a head when persons came from Judea to Antioch and insisted to new Gentile believers, "Unless you are circumcised according to the custom of Moses, you cannot be saved" (Acts 15:1). Paul and Barnabas rebutted "with no small dissension and debate." But the issue needed to be settled, and so they went to Jerusalem and requested that the leaders there make a judgment.

Did a Gentile need to become a Jew before one became a Christian? Was circumcision and kosher diet necessities for faith? As Theodore Ferris noted, ". . . the question had dynamite in it: . . . Is Christianity a national religion or a universal one?"[11] At the same time there was a question for the longtime Jewish Christians. Up to now, they had kept their dietary practices, which meant they ate with no one who did not. Were there to be two "separate but equal" churches in the future?

Apostles and elders met and debated for a long time. Both sides thoroughly expressed their beliefs and opinions. Peter recalled how the Spirit led him to the Roman Cornelius and his conversion. Then, there was silence. In time, Paul and Barnabas told of the signs and wonders God had done among the Gentiles during their travels.

---

11. Ferris, "Exposition on Acts," 196.

Finally, James the Just, brother of Jesus, witness to the resurrection—and a devout practicing Jewish believer—spoke. He suggested that "we should not trouble those Gentiles who are turning to God" but should ask them to conform to a few basic dietary observances that are most basic to Jewish observance and to remain sexually pure.

They also decided to send a letter informing the Christians in Antioch of this decision and to send respected members of their community along with Paul and Barnabas to interpret the letter and encourage them in the faith.

In this council, there was compromise. There were important concessions made by each side on a subject where all had deep convictions. In the end they listened to each other and to the Spirit and made a decision with which they could live. It was also a decision in which the gospel could flourish.

Conflict in the Corinthian Letters

When we move from Acts to the various letters in the latter portion of the New Testament, we find constant references to conflict. Even in the letter to the beloved and vital Philippian church, Paul early urges his readers to make his joy complete "be of the same mind, having the same love, being in full accord and of one mind" (Phil 2:2). Toward the end of the letter, he urges beloved coworkers Euodia and Synteche "to be of the same mind in the Lord" (4:2). He also asks a loyal companion to help them reconcile in the light of their history of sacrificial ministry and of their both having their "names in the book of life."

When we turn to Paul's correspondence with the Corinthians, there is conflict on nearly every page. After he finishes his opening greetings, Paul appeals "that all of you be in agreement and that there be no divisions among you, but that you be united in the same mind and the same purpose" (1Cor 1:10). The conflicts at Corinth appear to be many faceted. Early in the letter (1Cor 1:11–17), the church seems to have divided into factions of loyalty to various leaders who have visited the church and made a contribution to its life. At other points, they have asked Paul for advice on issues that were dividing them, and yet at other points, they resist Paul's authority as an apostle.

In all these struggles with the Corinthians, and struggles on their behalf, Paul delicately balances the authority of Christ, of himself as a spokesman on behalf of Christ, and of the Corinthian congregation, who must sort out the competing claims and make its own decisions. On a few occasions, it is Paul against the congregation; for the most part, he is attempting to help them deal with their own dilemmas.

The manner in which Paul helps them with their conflicts varies from issue to issue. Usually, his attitude is that of a gentle older brother, sometimes even encouraging them to reduce their high opinion of him. "Was Paul crucified for you? Or were you baptized in the name of Paul?" (1 Cor 1:13). He will not hesitate to tell them what he believes is a word from the Lord on the issues they are facing (and thus how they should settle some conflict). At other times he will admit, "I have no command from the Lord, but I give my opinion as one who by the Lord's mercy is trustworthy" (1Cor 7:25).

Once in a while, Paul changes from gentle brother to stern father. For example, in 1 Corinthians 5:3–5, he responds to the outrage of their complacency as regards an act of sexual immorality: ". . . I have already pronounced judgment in the name of the Lord Jesus on the man who has done such a thing. . . ."[12]

There are probably fragments of at least four letters from Paul in First and Second Corinthians. In this series of letters with the Corinthians, Paul also models that conflict is a process in a relationship, not the end of the relationship. In some of the later correspondence, he confesses to "much distress and anguish of heart and . . . many tears" (2 Cor 2:4) during the worst of the conflict. He also urges them to restore the one who has been disciplined (possibly the man in 1 Cor 5 about whom he spoke so harshly?).

Paul also makes clear that conflict can be transformative. At the end of this heart-wrenching struggle for all concerned, his writing soars to the heights of the joy of reconciliation and of becoming new creation (2 Cor 5:16–21). Quite possibly, the joy of restored human relationships within the church helped him understand and grasp even more profoundly the joy of reconciliation with our God! We will return to those writings shortly.

Conflict With the Galatians

If Paul's role in the Corinthian conflict was mainly that of mediator, in his letter to the Galatian church, he is clearly advocate for one position

---

12. I am indebted to David Bartlett's discussion of Paul's method of conflict intervention in *Ministry in the New Testament,* 31–39.

against another. While church leaders in the mother church in Jerusalem had settled the question of Gentile Christians (recorded in Acts 15 and discussed above), not all accepted that conclusion, and conflict over it broke out again and again. This phenomenon of a conflict not staying settled happens with many church situations.

This very same conflict erupted in Galatia, and Paul was outraged. In this letter, he rushes through the opening greeting and prayer, and says nothing nice about them, as would be customary. Instead he immediately writes, "I am astonished that you are so quickly deserting the one who called you in the grace of Christ and are turning to another gospel—not that there is another gospel" (Gal 1:6–7).

In quick order, he defends his authority as an apostle; tells the story of his conversion; and describes the decision and affirmation from the elders in Jerusalem (from Acts 15). He does this almost grudgingly—the truth of the grace of Christ should be so self-evident that it needs no bolstering from anyone else!

After talking about some other experiences, he restates the gospel in clear and stark terms (Gal 2:15–21). "For if justification comes through the law, then Christ died for nothing."

Passionately he cries out, "You foolish Galatians! Who has bewitched you?" (3:1). He goes through analogies and an exploration of why the law was given at all, and offers an allegory of Hagar and Sarah. All of this would be accepted and recognized methods of carrying on a thorough discussion and dispute. At the conclusion of this allegory, he cries out, "For freedom Christ has set us free. Stand firm, therefore, and do not submit again to a yoke of slavery" (Gal 5:1). He then appeals to them personally, recalling that though he came to them with a physical infirmity: "You did not scorn or despise me, but welcomed me as an angel of God, as Christ Jesus . . . you would have torn out your eyes and given them to me. Have I now become your enemy by telling you the truth?" Then he turns to a motherly metaphor: "My little children, for whom I am again in the pain of childbirth until Christ is formed in you . . . I am perplexed about you" (Gal. 4:14–19).

Once in a while, Paul speaks harshly about those who present a different view. For the most part, he engages heart and head, personal testimony and their relational history to convince these folks back. He concludes by calling them to their first belief and love, and to fruits of the Spirit. Then he concludes with a prayer, "May the grace of our Lord Jesus Christ be with your spirit" (Gal 6:18).

We don't know for sure how this particular controversy came out. Paul as a contestant in an all important church conflict shows us that it is right to argue with great energy and force for what we believe is right and to use every legitimate means of persuasion at our disposal.

It may be in conflict that our deepest convictions come most clear. Indeed, we can be grateful for the controversy in Galatia. It occasioned a powerful, normative statement of the heart of the gospel of freedom in Christ!

A Word from Ephesians

We now turn from studies of conflicts in the early church to a word about anger and conflict among believers. In Ephesians 4, there is given a series of words of guidance about the life of the Christian believer. Verses 25–27 speak to the subject of anger: "So then, putting away falsehood, let all of us speak the truth to our neighbors, for we are members of one another." Not only in the large issues of which we have been speaking, but in the daily contacts, our clear vision needs to be of our community, one body in Christ. And we are to maintain that membership of one another by abandoning falsehood and speaking the truth—even if it must be the hard truth as Paul did with the Galatians. The passage continues, "Be angry and do not sin; do not let the sun go down on your anger, and do not make room for the devil." The angers and conflicts of the day are to be dealt with promptly, day by day. Such anger is normal, but unattended, pushed under, ignored, it can fester and make room for discord, thus giving room for the devil! So deal with your conflicts promptly, for we are members one of another.

Carroll Saussy notes that when we combine these words from Ephesians with those of Jesus from Matthew 5 we are guided to three steps: "[F]irst, recognize the anger; second, direct it to its source; and third, seek reconciliation."[13] This is difficult to do, and to follow this guidance may be filled with conflict and pain. But if we, as the passage instructs, "speak the truth in love," it is the way through conflict that has integrity and hope.

Incidentally, in these very letters we have been exploring where anger-conflict is being negotiated so sensitively, there are also lists of

13. Saussy, *Gift of Anger*, 110.

vices, and these always include anger. For example, in Galatians 5:19–21 we read: "Now the works of the flesh are obvious: fornication, impurity, licentiousness, idolatry, sorcery, enmities, strife, jealousy, anger, quarrels, dissensions, factions, envy, drunkenness, carousing, and things like these." Other lists are found in 2 Corinthians 12:20 and Colossians 3:8—these also include anger. However, we must quickly add that the context of such lists makes clear that the anger condemned is the kind that destroys community, not the kind they are expressing to each other as they try to restore community.

Jesus, the Ultimate Reconciler, Agent of God's Shalom

So what have we learned in this overview? Hopefully, we have at least "normalized" anger and conflict, seeing them present among God's people in every age. Also, we have seen examples and been given guidance on a variety of ways to resolve conflict helpfully. But there is more. We have also been pointed to the one who holds us together in the midst of our difficulties with each other. Consider these foundational verses:

- "For he [Christ] is our peace; in his flesh he has made both groups into one and has broken down the dividing wall, that is, the hostility between us" (Eph 2:14);

- "For in him [Christ] all the fullness of God was pleased to dwell, and through him God was pleased to reconcile to himself all things, whether on earth or in heaven by making peace through his blood on the cross" (Col 1:19–20); and

- Paul also wrote in the glow of reconciliation with those Corinthians whose struggle so had so engaged him, "So if anyone is in Christ, there is a new creation: everything old has passed away; see, everything has become new! All this is from God who reconciled us to himself through Christ and has given us the ministry of reconciliation" (2 Cor 5:17–18).

In these conflicts in the New Testament church, the authority, the unifying principle, the irreducible core are all one and the same—God in Christ. God who acted uniquely in Christ binds us together in our various conflicts. God in Christ is the ultimate source of appeal in any conflict. God in Christ (and the free salvation by grace through faith that God offers) are the core convictions and beliefs we will not compromise.

Anger, Conflict, and Reconciliation in the Bible

God in Christ has not only reconciled dissident parties already, but ultimately wills the reconciliation of all to Godself and to each other.

Bound together with our great God, we can find ways through any conflicts that come, for Christ is our peace.

QUESTIONS AND ACTIVITIES FOR GROUP REFLECTION

1. Which of the biblical accounts of conflict and reconciliation touched you most deeply? Which answered questions you have about Christians and conflict? Which provided either models of reconciling conflict or specific guidance on conflict? Which, if any, inspired you?

2. In this brief overview of conflict and reconciliation in the Bible, what that you treasure did I leave out? What other texts and accounts would you have included? What would these have added to the exploration?

3. What do you learn for your life as you read about Jesus and conflict in the gospels?

4. What do you learn about Christians and conflict as you read 1–2 Corinthians? As you read Galatians? Ephesians?

5. What has this Bible study added to the discoveries made in the first three chapters of this book (about the gifts of anger, transforming possibilities, and barriers to the healing power of anger and conflict)?

5

Beyond Conflict about the Bible: A Beginning Dialogue

Another important task is to understand each other's approach to and interpretation of scripture. Interpretation of the Bible is not only one of the places where we sometimes differ; it is also often the source of many of our other conflicts. So exploring ways of interpretation may be one of the topics where we will gain the most. It may clarify why we read the Bible as we do and also help us hear and understand another who reads the Bible differently. Out of this, we may find ways where we can jointly explore what is the Bible's message for us as we work on difficult issues.

FOR YOUR PERSONAL OR GROUP WORSHIP

Scripture

Thy word is a lamp unto my feet, and a light unto my path. (Ps 119:105 KJV)

All scripture is inspired by God and is useful for teaching, for reproof, for correction, and for training in righteousness, so that everyone who belongs to God may be proficient, equipped for every good work. (2 Tim 3:16–17)

A Word to Ponder

The great Protestant theologian Karl Barth says that reading the Bible is like looking out of the window and seeing everybody on the street shading their eyes with their hands and gazing up into the sky toward something which is hidden from us by the roof.

They are pointing up. They are speaking strange words. They are very excited. Something is happening which we can't see happening. Or something is about to happen. Something beyond our comprehension has caught them up and is seeking to lead them on "from land to land for strange, intense, uncertain, and yet mysteriously well-planned service." (Frederick Buechner)[1]

The Bible is inherently the live word of God, revealing the character and will of God, and empowering us for an alternative life in the world.... I know that finally the Bible is forceful and consistent in its main theological claim. It expresses the conviction that the God who created the world in love redeems the world in suffering and will consummate the world in joyous well being. That flow of conviction about God's self-disclosure in the Bible is surely the main claim of the apostolic faith, a claim upon which the church fundamentally agrees. That fundamental agreement is, of course, the beginning of the conversation and not its conclusion; but it is a deep and important starting point. (Walter Brueggemann)[2]

FOR YOUR THOUGHT AND REFLECTION

As we search for loving, respectful dialogue across our differences, we will need to talk about our reading and interpreting of the Bible. Why do people study the Bible and come out with quite different conclusions on the same subject? Is it because some of us are in error and others of us possess the truth on the matter under consideration? Or may there be something to be learned from these differences? Is there any way we can dialogue about something as deeply emotional as how we see the Bible and its ethical claims on us?

For years, I have attempted to help students in my ethics classes carry on just such a conversation. These students have come from a wide range of denominations, backgrounds, and convictions about the Bible. We have discovered that it is important to be able to identify our assumptions about the Bible and name our ways of approaching and interpreting the Bible. When we can do that, it increases the possibilities that we can talk with each other across those differences and difficulties.

---

1. Frederick Buechner, *Wishful Thinking: A Theological ABC,* 9. The quote is from Karl Barth's *The Word of God and the Word of Men*, 63.
2. Walter Brueggemann, "Biblical Authority; a Personal Reflection," 15.

We have learned that in order to do this, we need to be as clear as we can be on four topics: (A) On what beliefs and convictions do we agree as we approach the Bible? (B) What else do we have in common as we study and interpret the Bible? (C) Where do we differ with each other as regards the Bible? (D) How can we use this information to increase our chances of enriching dialogue with each other?

I am going to offer some thoughts on each of these topics, and I invite your careful and critical evaluation. It is not so important that we agree as to what is on these lists, as that we begin a process of reflection and conversation on these topics. In so doing, we move our approach to the Bible from unconscious and instinctive to conscious and visible. Then, maybe, good things can happen in our dialogue with each other about the Bible's teachings on difficult topics.

On What Do We Agree?

Here are some beliefs about the Bible that I believe most of us Christian people hold in common:

1. The Bible is a means by which we encounter God. Whether it is study in the company of others or a solitary person taking up this book and reading it, there is often a transforming experience. Persons not only learn about God; they encounter God, either in a new or in a fresh and renewing way. As 1 Thess 4:9 tells us, we are "God taught." To follow the analogy from the Karl Barth quote at the chapter's beginning, when we read the Bible we come outside to see what people are pointing at. And we see the reality as well.

2. The Bible is a book of the acts of God. This book describes God creating and redeeming God's people—again and again. Not only has God redeemed in exodus, in atonement, in resurrection, but also God's redeeming work is not yet finished. However dark the times, we are hopeful, because the Bible witnesses to a redeeming God who is still acting with God's creation or God's people.

3. The Bible reveals how God's people are to live. The acting, redeeming God calls people into covenant relationship. In grateful response, God's people are given commandments and other guidance as to how to keep their part of the covenant. At least the

broad guidelines of this covenant living—Ten Commandments, Jesus's love commandments, and more—are quite clear.

4. As John Robinson promised Christian folk leaving for the "New World," God has more light and truth yet to break forth out of God's Holy Word. The Bible is a living Word, and God uses it to speak to people in new and different ages. Throughout the history of the church, over and again, the church has been born anew, its flame rekindled by hearing a fresh word from the Bible. It may well be that there is a renewing word of guidance for those who attend to the Word with open hearts and minds.

5. Witness from the Bible builds community. I recall with gratitude times when I have been worshipping with folks who see many things differently than I do. Then a preacher stands and speaks out of careful study and encounter with the Bible. That preacher brings a new word, alive with truth and conviction. I came suspicious and distant, but I am touched. Through a person's witness of that one's encounter with the Word, community is created. Harmony feels possible. Giving and hearing witness of persons who have come to the Bible with open hearts and minds is a building up experience.

6. God renews God's people through the Bible. I am aware of a church, where in response to a pastor's faithful and rigorous preaching, people came and asked him to help them hear the Bible that way. And so a small covenant group met to explore the teachings of Jesus. They had some very simple ground rules. They agreed they would try very hard to discover exactly what Jesus said, and, as best they could, comprehend what he meant. They also agreed that whether each person in the group chose to obey or not, they would not kid themselves. They would not pretend they were obeying that teaching of Jesus if they were not. The study stretched from weeks into months, and then years. Commitment of individual members grew in depth and permeated their church and community. Story after story could be told of churches being renewed when the Bible is studied honestly, and in depth.

7. The Bible is to be taken seriously. Encounters with the God of the Bible are too powerful and meaningful, guidance from

the Bible is too reliable, and the renewing force of the Bible is too prevalent for it to be otherwise. We followers of Christ are people of the Book. If we meet at all, we will meet over the Book, our Bibles in our hearts and in our hands.

There may be other items that could be on this list. However, I trust that these convictions about the Bible are widely shared and accepted.

What Else Do We Have In Common?

There is a Chinese proverb that states, "Ninety percent of what we see lies *behind* our eyes."[3] And so this is yet another thing we have in common, that we have much behind our eyes that we see as we approach the Bible.

1. We each come out of a church, a faith community, and the influence of strong leaders within that community. Those leaders, that church may have had issues on which they took a strong stand. There may have been comments about people who believed or behaved otherwise. Every one of us comes to the Bible with the influence of the churches and religious leaders of a lifetime behind our eyes.

2. Many of us probably come to the Bible with issues and causes that are near to our heart. Each of us comes from a particular ethnic group, gender, social class, educational experience, and political stance; these inevitably influence how we see the Bible. We may have pain and hurt around a given issue. Or we may have a very strong conviction about something. We do not leave this behind when we come to the Bible to search for what it says on this topic. In all honesty, many of us look for something that will support us in our previous convictions. And, we are usually not disappointed!

3. We also come with vivid, attitude forming experiences of our own, and we have heard equally vivid stories from others. Every one of us has a history, which is at the same time sacred, whole, and broken. At times each of us is confused as to what of our history is sacred and whole, and what of our history is broken.

---

3. Quoted in Bruce C. Birch and Larry L. Rasmussen, *Bible and Ethics in the Christian Life*, 90.

In this connection, it is worth recalling David G. Myers's statement. He did a takeoff on Mark Twain's statement that there were three kinds of lies—lies, damn lies, and statistics. Myers countered that with apologies to Mark Twain, "there are three kinds of lies—lies, damned lies, and vivid but misleading anecdotes."[4]

Those vivid but misleading stories/anecdotes may be ours—yours and mine. But how are we to sort out what of our experience is revelatory, a reliable guide as we approach scripture and seek the right way? How are we to know that our experiences may be important, but a minor and potentially misleading part of a larger truth?

We may not ever know, but we will probably trust our own experience more than anything else will. And so these experiences comprise a powerful part of that which is behind our eyes as we come to scripture.

What we have in common is that for all of us, much of what we see is behind our eyes. Where we differ is what is behind our eyes—those life stories with all their influences that have brought us to the present moment.

All of these aspects of our experience influence the way we encounter the Bible; to what parts we turn first, what we hear. This may be quite different from someone with a different set of experiences.

While this may make dialogue about divisive issues in the Bible difficult, it does not make it impossible. It does mean that we need to pay attention to these matters. Each of us needs to be in touch with one's own history, experience and convictions. Each of us needs also carefully to listen to the history, experience, and convictions of the person before us.

Where Do We Differ?

In addition to coming to the Bible from quite different histories, there are some more specific differences that may complicate our dialogue.

1. We may disagree as to what areas the Bible is authoritative. Some of us see the Bible as authoritative in all matters: faith, practice, science, history, geography, and psychology, among others. Others of us see the Bible as being addressed to a specific people in a specific age, speaking to the cultural norms for that

---

4. David G. Myers, *The American Paradox: Spiritual Hunger in an Age of Plenty*, xiii.

day and in that age. Those of us who use this approach are not as likely to attribute authority to what the Bible says on matters where recent research has yielded new information or insights.

2. We may also have differences about how to interpret the cultural and social settings in which the Bible was written and the impact of that on the written word. It was written in cultures much different than our own, millennia ago. What do we make of these cultural influences in the Bible? Some of us say that it is neither possible nor necessary to try to sort this out. Accept and believe the Bible and what it commands. Others insist that we should not absolutize the culture in which the Bible was written nor the Bible when it expresses these cultural beliefs and practices. We have the task of distinguishing what was written for that age and what was written for all ages.[5]

3. In the same connection, we may disagree as to whether seeming disparities in the Bible are real or only apparent, perhaps awaiting further discovery. These items may be over historical detail, or they may be teachings and commands on ethical issues.

4. In a similar vein, we may have a variety of viewpoints as we attempt faithfully to interpret and practice Bible teachings that are quite clear. For example, the Bible authorizes the death penalty for at least seventeen different offences. These include disobedience to parents, striking of parents, Sabbath breaking, having intercourse during menstruation, and blasphemy, as well as murder.

How does a faithful interpreter of the Bible apply this information? Advocate the death penalty for all that the Bible mentions? Advocate the death penalty but only for a few heinous crimes? Advocate the death penalty, but first consider if the Bible's teachings on mercy (from God's treatment of the first murderer, Cain through Jesus's acts of forgiveness) would mitigate the penalty? Or, read the passages on mercy as a new commandment and promote abolishing capital punishment?[6]

---

5. For the former view—the culture and Bible are inextricably intertwined—see Richard B. Hays, *The Moral Vision of the New Testament*. For the latter view—one should not absolutize the culture in which the Bible was written—see Virginia Ramey Mollenkott, *Men, Women, and the Bible*.

6. For a thoughtful discussion of these options, see Glen H. Stassen, "Biblical

5. We may disagree on the importance of the amount of attention paid to an issue, within the Bible, that is, the frequency with which it is mentioned. If a topic is mentioned infrequently without elaboration, does the Bible's teachings on that have the same force and validity as those teachings that are referred to time and again, elaborated and nuanced? Some of us say yes, some of us say no.

6. We may have differences as to how we perceive the unity of scriptures. Some of us hear the Bible speaking with one voice from start to finish. The God who spoke in creation, also spoke in the Torah, in the Psalms and Proverbs, through the Prophets and through the Christ.

    Others of us believe we perceive a progression. These folks feel they see a development of the ability of people to receive and apply God's guidance over the nearly 2000-year period the Bible covers. This latter group is apt to look for reinterpretations of earlier teachings in the prophets and particularly in the unconditional love articulated by Jesus the Christ. When they feel they find this, they give greater credence to the reinterpretation, which they believe is both later, and a more mature perceiving of God's revelation.

7. We may disagree over what sources of guidance there are, in addition to the Bible. Even more, we may disagree as to the significance of these sources of guidance and how they are to be utilized. At least four other sources of guidance are sometimes cited in guiding decisions:

    a) church, including one's local faith community, one's denomination, the church of the ages, and the ecumenical church;

    b) one's personal experience, including one's conscience that develops as one seeks God's guidance and internalizes the important influences, teachings, and events of one's life;

    c) the findings of modern science, including the science of persons; and

---

Teachings on Capital Punishment," in *Capital Punishment: A Reader*, edited by Glen H. Stassen, 119–30.

d) the guidance of the Holy Spirit, revealing to God's people new truth in new and as yet unfaced circumstances.

If all these resources are available to aid in moral deliberation, then which are valid? Which should be consulted? What priorities should there be among them? And what credence or authority should be given them?

Some of us answer that the Bible is our supreme norm. Information from these other sources might be helpful, but it is always supplemental information and does not alter the Bible's teachings.

Others of us see all these sources of guidance as God given and attempt a "round table discussion" among these sources, including the Bible. Open-end coherence, feedback loops between experience, Bible, and all these sources of guidance rest guide us in our decisions.

8. We may not mean the same thing when we speak of the Bible as "inspired." For some of us, the Bible as the inspired word of God has a clear and straightforward meaning. It means that God spoke the words of the Bible (through faithful servants) and that whatever we read in the Bible are God's words to us. Dennis Hollinger states this view well. "The inspiration of Scripture was not a dictation from heaven but embodied both divine and human elements. Nonetheless, God was providentially at work in both the revelatory events and the spoken or written word in such a way that what we have is what God intended."[7]

For others of us, the word "inspired" is closer to the root meaning of the word, "in-breathed." The Bible is in-breathed with God's spirit. God is found there. God is met there. God guides there. God renews and invites there. God inspires there. But for those of us who read this way, inspiration is a more mysterious, indirect process than the former group finds, less likely to provide clear guidance and directives.

---

7. Dennis P. Hollinger, *Choosing the Good: Christian Ethics in a Complex World*, 152.

How then can we dialogue across these differences?

If I have accurately described our differences in approaching the scriptures, we have quite a task in learning to talk to each other. I suggest a few steps to guide us in this tremendously important work of beginning this dialogue.

1. Be prepared for uncomfortable and disturbing discoveries and revelations as we carry on this conversation with the Bible and with each other. In an essay on biblical hermeneutics, David Scholer writes, "The New Testament image (Heb 4:12) of the word of God as '. . . living and active [and] sharper than any doubled edged sword . . .' (NIV) indicates that no one should or can ever have a 'safe' hermeneutic which 'boxes' the Bible, and then God, into the categories which we choose for our theological security and personal comfort."[8] We are to come to this conversation, ready to change if we are so led.

2. Avoid pejorative, "put down" language of approaches that are not your own. It is pejorative to say that another's approach is "simplistic," or "simple minded." It is also pejorative to say "I have a higher view of scripture than you do." One side may be tempted to call the other "unthinking" and the other may be equally tempted to describe the other side from them as "unbelieving." However, such labels only complicate and heat up an already difficult discussion. In Mark 3:22, Jesus's opponents engaged in this very act. They said, "He has Beelzebul, and by the ruler of demons he casts out demons." What a tragedy! Think of what they missed by resorting to name calling rather than considering who was really before them and what was happening before their very eyes!

    Instead, each of us needs to search for accurate and objective ways to describe one's own and another's approach to scripture. Perhaps describing oneself and then interviewing another about each of the points in the previous three sections can give one those terms that make for civil discussion.

3. Respect your own and another's way of dialoguing with scripture. Each of us interprets scripture as we do partly as a result of

---

8. David M. Scholer, "Unreasonable Thoughts on the State of Biblical Hermeneutics: Reflections of a New Testament Exegete," 140.

our history and partly as a result of what has spoken most vitally to us when we came to more systematic study of the Bible. None of us is completely without reason why we interpret scripture as we do, and none of us is entirely objective and rational. (We probably couldn't be if we wanted to, for we are speaking of the Source Book guiding us to the One who is Life indeed!)

And, there is infinite variation among us. We cannot (at least we should not) put anyone in an "ideological box" simply out of hearing them say a few things about the Bible. Rather we need to hear that person's story about his/her encounter with the Bible, and therefore what it means to that person and how he/she interprets it.

4. Be aware that we need each other. Our discoveries may be more valid and more grounded, perhaps even more creative, if this dialogue happens. We may have already discovered how sterile and repetitive our conversations become when we speak only with people who agree with us. Discovery, inspiration, and insight may await me if I open myself to another member of the Body of Christ whose experience and approach to the Bible is quite different than mine.

5. Try out a method that most of us can find useful. In this connection, I offer the guidance of biblical scholar Brevard Childs. Childs asks, "How does the Bible aid the Christian in the making of concrete ethical decisions?" In response, he offers a two step process to obtain such guidance.

First, after stating the ethical dilemma as clearly as one can, a person "attempts to sketch the *full range* of the Biblical witnesses within the canonical context that have bearing on the subject at issue." Childs says that sketching the full range of all biblical witnesses helps a person determine whether there is a variety of responses-answers to the question we have addressed to scripture. In his words, we are attempting to "hear the complete scale of notes that are played," first in the original setting, and then in relationship to the other writings on the same topic in the whole canon. (While Childs describes this as done by an individual, this task might be better done by a group, all attempting to understand each relevant scriptural passage both in its own context and relationship to other passages.)

We need to take this step aware of the rich variety of forms of ethical guidance in the scriptures. Hollinger reminds us that there are least these types of resources: (a) casuistic law—case laws, if something happens, then this should be done; (b) apodictic laws—straightforward regulations in the form of divine commands; (c) principles—general foundational perspectives—duties, ideals, responsibilities, life orientations; (d) paradigms with implied ethical guidance, such as the Lordship of Christ, or sacrificial love; (e) moral examples and narratives (both positive and negative).[9] I would add (f) hymns, prayers, poetry, parables also with possible implied ethical application.

Second, seek to understand the *"inner movement* of the various witnesses" that have been found in the Bible. Childs suggests that there may well be a variety of patterns of movement one discovers in asking this second question. For example, one may find:

- One clear imperative throughout scripture, (for example the Bible's consistent command to love God and neighbor) or

- Two seemingly conflicting teachings needing some analysis and dialogue, (for example, the command to "obey God rather than man" and the command to obey the higher authorities) or

- A set of teachings in need of prioritizing (for example, the Bible's varied passages on sexuality or marriage) or

- Lack of clarity in everything except the outer limits, (for example, seeking biblical guidance on military conscription or the population explosion or problems of the middle east) or, perhaps,

- Total uncertainty in everything but the justifying grace of God and, therefore, freedom (such as how the church and the Christian live in a time of totalitarian extremes).[10]

Childs' two step process inviting careful biblical research on sensitive ethical issues is demanding, extensive, and exhaustive, to be sure. It asks of us time, effort, and discipline. However, done carefully and well, it may be a means to even more than is first apparent. We may be provided fresh revelation about the issue at hand. Even more, God may grant us

---

9. Hollinger, op. cit. 162–73.
10. Brevard Childs, *Biblical Theology in Crisis*, 123–38.

information about each other and lead us to deeper communion than we thought possible. Indeed, dialogue about scripture across our differences may be an occasion to claim that promise that God does indeed have more light and truth to break forth out of God's Holy Word.

QUESTIONS AND ACTIVITIES FOR GROUP REFLECTION

1. Take some time to reflect on how you came to view the Bible as you do. Who were the people who introduced you to the Bible? Who has inspired you by their study and knowledge of the Bible? Has anyone interpreted the Bible in a way that you felt led to reject? If so, who, and why?

2. List the items I suggest on which we agree. As you think of Christian friends with whom you sometimes have differences, do you concur on these items? If not, which ones would you not include? Are there other items about the Bible on which we agree that I failed to mention?

3. Did my suggestion that much of what we see comes from behind our eyes (our varied experiences and discoveries of the past) make sense to you? If so, what did it say to you? What lies behind your eyes as you read and interpret scripture?

4. List and discuss my suggested list of differences between Christian people on their understanding of scripture. Are there others? Can one have Christian fellowship and dialogue with folks who differ on these topics?

5. List and discuss my suggestions for carrying on dialogue across those differences. Which seem most helpful? Least helpful? What would you add?

6

The Purpose of the Church: A Search for Biblical Priorities

...As we come to such a place of mutual listening for God's voice within the Bible, there is a deep and profound question we must ask. What is the God of the Bible saying to the church about its mission in the twenty-first century? It may well be that a basic step to our deeper unity will be around that mission to which God calls us out of scripture...

FOR YOUR PERSONAL OR GROUP WORSHIP

Scripture

"Teacher, which commandment in the law is the greatest?" He said to him, "'You shall love the Lord your God with all your heart, and with all your soul, and with all your mind.' This is the greatest and first commandment. And the second is like it: 'You shall love your neighbor as yourself.' On these two commandments hang all the law and the prophets." (Matt 22:36–40)

...what does the Lord require of you,
but to do justice, and to love kindness,
and to walk humbly with your God? (Mic 6:8b)

A Word to Ponder

The purpose of the church is the increase among [all people] of the love of God and neighbor....

By love we mean at least these attitudes and actions: rejoicing in the presence of the beloved, gratitude, reverence, and loyalty toward him. Love is rejoicing over the existence of the beloved one; it is the desire that he be rather than not be; it is longing for his presence when he is absent. . . . Love is gratitude; it is thankfulness for the existence of the beloved. . . . Love is reverence: it keeps its distance even as it draws near. . . . Love is loyalty: it is the willingness to let the self be destroyed rather than that the other cease to be. . . . It is loyalty to the other's cause—to his loyalty. (H. Richard Niebuhr)[1]

FOR YOUR THOUGHT AND REFLECTION

I did a little survey in which I proved nothing but learned much. This survey is connected to the two reasons that led me to work on this book. On the one hand, I have deep feelings about this subject and wanted to offer my knowledge, information, and perspective to help other people work on it. On the other hand, I am also puzzled, perplexed and curious about what is happening to the church, and I want/need to know more myself.

And so I set about doing as many different kinds of research as I could. I read books, web sites, and periodicals; interviewed experts; reflected on my own experiences; went to workshops and seminars; and applied all this (and learned more) as I offered courses on related topics to my seminary students.

As helpful as all these were, I felt I could learn still more from yet another source—the people most affected by all this. And so I decided to gather opinions from church members and leaders who do not consider themselves experts. I wanted to know their beliefs about the primary mission of the church as well as their hopes for the church. My hunch was that if the church responded to a clear sense of God's call, both as to what it was to do and to be, our conflicts with each other would diminish considerably.

Thus, this chapter will be quite different from everything else in this book. I am going to describe for you this little survey I did, although I well know there is nothing scientific or precise either in the way I created the questionnaire or in the way I found those who responded. While it doesn't prove anything, it does raise some interesting thoughts and questions.

Here is the questionnaire I designed:

---

1. H. Richard Niebuhr, *The Purpose of the Church and Its Ministry*, 32.

The Purpose of the Church 85

Your Informed Opinion Please

You are a Christian, a church person, a leader, and a student-lover of the Bible. You are all of these things in the twenty-first century.

What do you believe to be the five most basic mandates in the Bible for the people of God today?

Or, to put it another way, as you study the Bible, what do you hear as God's most basic claims—expectations for the church today?

If the church were to reorder its priorities in the light of God's call to us out of scriptures, what would the five highest priorities be? (Your answer need not be in any order of priority within the five).

1.

2.

3.

4.

5.

That was the questionnaire. Before going any further, stop for a moment.

You, too, are invited to respond to this survey. Indeed, you are urged to look at item one in the "Questions and Activities for Group Discussion" at the end of this chapter. You may discover and learn more if you and others in your group or class answer the questionnaire before you read on and learn how others responded. Think about what you hear God saying out of scripture to the church today—the church of which you are a part in particular—as to what it is to do and be. When you have completed the questionnaire individually or as a group, or (it's a free country) decided not to, go on.

I must tell you that creating this questionnaire was much more difficult than I thought it would be. Unsure that I had asked my question clearly, I asked it three different ways (the second, third, and fourth sentences of the questionnaire). However, after much struggle and many rewrites, I went with it and started to circulate it.

My process was simply to use a "convenience sample." That is, I asked folks around me to give it some thought and respond. I passed it out to seminary students in my ethics classes, my seminary faculty colleagues, fellow pastors, friends, and adult Sunday School classes or seminars I was asked to lead. (Though it might have been interesting, I did not separate responses from faculty, students, pastors, lay persons. It would also be interesting to do this with youths and children, but I did not do that.) While I know that the folks who responded represent a wide spectrum of Christian thought, there is no claim that they are an adequate sampling of any given population.

When I presented the questionnaire, some would answer in a few moments, and hand it right back. Others found the questions to require deep thought, reflection, and pondering. Their responses came back weeks later, or not at all. Some would apologetically ask for another copy of the questionnaire—by the time they figured out what they wanted to say on it, they had lost the first one!

I passed out two hundred or so and received more than sixty responses. Here is a report of what these completed questionnaires contained. These are what these respondents believed were the highest biblical priorities-mandates for the twenty first century church. The priorities these people listed will be given in order of the frequency of response. While I won't attempt to give you precise numbers or percentages, every response given will be mentioned.

The two responses selected by the highest number of people closely followed the two greatest commandments Jesus gave us, as we recorded from Matthew 22 at the beginning of this chapter. These two were mentioned in some form on nearly every questionnaire.

The first mandate these people perceived is to love God. Persons added various comments, "with whole mind, heart, and strength . . . having no other gods before God . . . believe in the one true God of love."

With equal emphasis the respondents listed the mandate to love neighbor as self. Again, there was a variety of emphases and nuances in the answers: "Love as God loves . . . respecting diversity . . . love family friends, community, even enemies . . . love without regard to race, color, or background . . . accept all people and all differences . . . Let there be acceptance of one another." Sometimes in this connection, sometimes as a separate item on the list, several people listed the "Golden Rule,"—"Do unto others as you would have them do unto you" (Luke 7:31; see also Matt. 7:12).

In this, they were coming out at exactly the same place as H. Richard Niebuhr in his classic study of the purpose of the church and of ministry, which we quoted at the beginning of this chapter. "The purpose of the church is the increase among all people of the love of God and neighbor."

While these two responses-commands were nearly universally mentioned, the next was mentioned by at least two thirds of the respondents. It was the mandate to personal witness. This priority was also stated variously. "Go into the world and make disciples of the nations . . . advance the Word . . . tell the story of salvation . . . point to Jesus as the way the truth, and the life . . . accept Christ as Lord and Savior and be baptized."

Others spoke of other aspects of the mission to the world, for example, "To seek peace among the nations."

Then there were three answers that were each mentioned by about twenty percent of the respondents. One of these was Micah's summary of what the Lord requires of us, "to do justice, show mercy, and walk humbly with our God" (6:8).

Another of these was worship. "Express love of God through worship . . . worship and glorify God . . . worship in spirit and in truth."

Still another was the calling to be a servant people. One put it "United in service to the world." Still others offered specific thoughts as to where they discerned that servanthood should be expressed. "To care for the poor, the elderly, the ill at their point of need . . . to serve the 'least of these' . . . the first shall be last and the last first."

Next in frequency was a number of statements that an aspect of Scripture's call to us is not only to doing, but also to being, to character. There were some who spoke of the claim on the individual believer. "To be transformed by our faith . . . to express Christian character, the new way of life as a result of our faith . . . to live righteous and holy lives . . . through our living out of love and righteousness share the gospel with all . . . to seek first the kingdom of God . . . to imitate Christ . . . to seek the fruit of the spirit, love, joy, peace, kindness, goodness, faithfulness, gentleness, and self control . . . to advance and grow as a person into the image of God."

Closely related was a number of responses that identified a call for individuals to live well with each other, and for the church to be a community of harmony. "To live in dynamic relationship with God and others... have a special relationship with other believers... the church is to be united... to learn to forgive... to accept all people and all differences ... to show acceptance of one another."

There were a few responses that spoke of the call to develop a deep sense of stewardship/managership of all that God has entrusted to us. One spoke in general, "Live knowing God is creator of all and redeemer of humankind." One specifically mentioned being "wise and faithful stewards of God's creation." Another referred to financial resources, "To teach and hold a proper attitude toward money."

And there were a number of responses that could be included in any number of places above. "To pray... the first shall be last and the last first... you are accepted by grace through faith... teach... repent...."

That was the survey and what people said. Every single response given has been mentioned somewhere in the previous pages, as I attempted to group them together in various categories.

I never filled out my own questionnaire. It was probably good not to do so before I read the wide range of responses to it. And I must also confess I never saw a single completed questionnaire that had exactly the same responses I would have given. However, to keep my promise about not imposing my own views about issues in this book, I will not give my answers now. (I do freely express my passion for a redemptive, transforming use of anger and conflict, for a more healing dialogue, and for a deeper unity among us.)

After investing this much time and effort myself, and asking for the time, thought, and opinions of many others, I now give consideration to some questions about this investigation. (And yes, I still remember my disclaimer that this is not a scientific survey in any sense of the word.) What did I hope to learn? Were there any surprises? What did I actually learn from this information gathering?

What did I hope to learn? I wanted to know if people saw any connection between the Bible's most basic mandates for the church and the issues that are dominating the church's agenda and energy. The issues I hear debated divisively are mostly around styles of worship, abortion, and homosexuality, although the leadership of women, church building programs and who is accountable when things do not go well are also frequent topics.

If at all, these issues were mentioned indirectly. Worship was spoken of, but the answers were about the purpose and goal of worship, not about the style with which it would be conducted. There were many answers about Christian character, and these are not unrelated to how people conduct their sexual lives.

Still, I think it must be said that many of our conflicts are about sexual matters and no one heard a priority Bible mandate about sex. But perhaps that is to oversimplify matters. On this topic, Richard Mouw comments helpfully in his book, *Uncommon Decency*. As an evangelical leader, he often hears the criticism that the only social issues evangelicals are concerned about are "pornography, homosexuality, abortion, divorce, fornication, adultery." He concedes there is a grain of truth to this criticism, and then goes on to say:

> But I am not ready to concede that our intense interest in sexual matters is simply misguided. Sexuality is a very important part of our created nature. The Bible makes this clear in its opening pages: God's first words to the man and woman are "Be fruitful and multiply" (Gen. 1:28). And the very first thing that happens to Adam and Eve after they eat the forbidden fruit is that they notice their nakedness and try to cover themselves.
>
> Sex and reproduction play a basic role in the human drama. We humans are complex and vulnerable beings, and our complexity and vulnerability are nowhere more obvious than in our sexuality. A society that is fundamentally confused about the rights and wrongs of sex cannot be very healthy.[2]

Mouw goes on to suggest ways that people can address sexual issues civilly—with penitence, humility, care for persons, and grace. In this, he makes two very significant points for our discussion: that sexual issues are an important and worthy part of the conversation and debates Christians need to have with each other; and that this can be done in a civil manner.

That is true. But we must also acknowledge that the energy and highest priorities of those who responded to my questionnaire were given to other matters. If these respondents perceived the Bible's man-

---

2. Richard J. Mouw. *Uncommon Decency: Christian Civility in an Uncivil World*, 82.

dates correctly, we of the Christian community are off track in what is demanding our greatest attention and often draining our energy.

Of course, there may be another reason that none of those who returned my questionnaire spoke of sexual issues—they may have written the church off as having anything civil or helpful to say on the subject of sex. I doubt that is the case, but it could be true. I suspect the greater wisdom is that as important as sexual matters and the church's helpful moral counsel on these issues are, there are even more basic purposes to which God calls the church out of scripture. That is what my respondents perceived and were saying.

Were there any other surprises? Yes, in addition to the fact that no one directly mentioned the issues that are often hotly contested among church people, I was also surprised that there was so little mention of justice for gender or race, ecology, peace making, or reducing violence.

What did I learn from this focused conversation with this group of people? There's a vague uneasiness that I asked the questions so broadly that I didn't learn anything. I did ask immense questions; people gave equally broad answers; and in my reporting them, I grouped the responses even more broadly! There were no questions about specific applications of the basic mandates, nor about the settings in which they most need to be followed. The survey was a good first step, but for greater benefit, more refined research on many levels is needed. I learned how much more we need to know about the minds, perceptions, and commitments of church people.

Still, there are some discoveries to be made. One learning is that, in my opinion, the wide range of church people who responded to the questionnaire had a firm grasp of many important biblical mandates for today's and tomorrow's church. If we come back to the basics they located and put first things first, we will be able to keep our controversies more in perspective.

Still another discovery is that though a beginning and elementary step, the survey posed valid questions that led to substantive responses. Questions can be educative and revealing. The ones raised here are important and stimulated people to do some important theological probing (albeit very basic probing) about the nature and purpose of the church.

Still another discovery, however, is that if all sixty who answered this questionnaire were in the same church and tried to work out the highest mission priorities for their church, they'd have quite a task. That is because there was tremendous diversity among the responses.

How delightful it will be when churches decide to give this a try. Let's seek to discover what God's most basic will is for us today and tomorrow. This search can take many forms, but it is important that we undertake it.

My little questionnaire might open the question with your church, but don't stop there. This might help you locate the most basic Bible passages that need deep, urgent and prayerful attention as you listen for God's call.

There are other steps that may be helpful. For example, recall your church's history, its original calling, when God's blessing was most clearly upon it. Or, perhaps, you need to hear from persons who are carrying on front line ministries with "the least of these" (whoever they are) in your community.

In the next chapter, I will point you toward those who are helping churches to use the gifts of discernment to rediscover calling and make major decisions. You might want to learn and engage that discernment process. And later, in the final chapter, I am going to let my moral imagination loose—and invite you to explore your moral imagination as well—about many cries of need from the world to which a renewed and united church could respond. Consideration of that chapter might open new vistas for you and the church of which you are a part.

Form study groups, pore over our Bibles, give ourselves to prayerful discernment, and walk around our community, observing and listening. Then come together and talk about what we believe most deeply to be the primary callings of our churches out of all of this.

Let each of us feel free to present what we have discovered with all the vigor we possess. Listen carefully to others as they do the same. When that happens, there will be 21st century versions of those debates we mentioned in chapter four from the book of Acts. What a time that will be!

QUESTIONS AND ACTIVITIES FOR GROUP REFLECTION

1. Fill out the questionnaire yourself. If you are studying this book with a Sunday School class or other small group, circulate the questionnaire among all the members. Collect them and com-

pile them. Compare your personal response or your group's responses with that of the people I surveyed. How are your responses similar? How are they different?

2. In light of the discussion above, where do you put the debate on sexual issues as regards biblical priorities? Most important? Significant but not primary? Not very important? On what basis do you answer as you do?

3. The chapter suggests the church is "off track" as far as putting its main attention, energy, and resources into its highest priorities. Do you agree? If so, what are your thoughts for getting the church "on track" again?

4. What are the methods your church utilizes for identifying or refocusing its mission and purpose? What contributes to the success of those methods? What could make them even more effective?

5. What do you think about my description of what I learned from doing this exercise? What have you learned from doing it?

Part Three

Vistas of Change and Reconciliation

7

Parables of Hope and Promise

. . . Fellow saints and servants, there are also inspiring examples to guide and encourage us as we seek the path through conflict to a greater harmony in the church. Persons with radically different views have looked for and discovered Common Ground, holy ground. Others have discovered how to make church gatherings— boards and business meetings—Worshipful Work. And leaders who began helping to heal the strife in the emerging nation of South Africa have gone many other places in the world helping persons work on divisive issues. They now offer the church their methods of Peace Building and Conflict Transformation. The visions they had and the strategies they discovered may be used of God to inspire, guide, and stimulate us to find equally creative ways . . .

FOR YOUR PERSONAL OR GROUP WORSHIP

Scripture

"Blessed are the peacemakers, for they will be called children of God."(Matt 5:9)

"Do not be conformed to this world, but be transformed by the renewing of your minds, so that you may discern what is the will of God—what is good and acceptable and perfect." (Rom 12:2)

A Word to Ponder

Today is an in-between time for the church, between the past, when the church was firmly established in Christendom, and an unclear future for the church. Today is a time for redefinition; it is a time for the church to listen to its stories, to talk about its direction and identity, and to patiently discern the shape of its future life and ministry. (Danny E. Morris and Charles M. Olsen)[1]

FOR YOUR THOUGHT AND REFLECTION

In this chapter, we move on to a new stage in our conversation. From reflection on anger-conflict and exploration of the Bible on these topics, we now turn to contemporary stories and examples. These are about people who have claimed these possibilities and who work on controversies in healing ways.

I will tell stories of three such experiments. These stories/parables have widely varied subjects. One is about the pioneering efforts of women and men to talk with each other across broad differences, seeking common ground. A second is about a movement that arose in an attempt to bring spirituality and spiritual enrichment to church boards. A third is a conflict transformation process first developed to assist a struggling, emerging nation deal with its many local conflicts, but it is also helpful to communities and churches around the world.

These are rather complex stories/parables. With each, I speak of the issue or problem they addressed; describe some of their most basic concepts, methods and procedures; and tell of what they have achieved. I tell these stories, all too briefly, with the hope that they will inspire hope and stimulate creativity. I must tell you that two of these three are no longer in existence, at least not in the form they once were. Their influence lives on in the practices of those who learned from them and in the inspiration of people who were touched by them, and this includes me.

People of Good Will Sought—and Found—Common Ground

One of the most divisive issues, not only for Christians and churches but also for society at large, has been abortion. Well aware that this topic is often the occasion of bitter and violent confrontations, there are a number of people who have longed for, looked for, and worked for a better way.

In the early 1990's, one of those groups—the Common Ground Network for Life and Choice—came into being on a shoestring budget with the goal of transforming the abortion debate in America. One of its first tasks was to develop a working model for providing community level pro-choice/pro-life dialogue in Buffalo, New York. They also became

---

1. Morris and Olsen, *Discerning God's Will Together*, 12.

aware of similar efforts in other cities, and so they gathered participants from these that they could learn from each other. At that gathering, it was also agreed that a "central office" would be useful to link local efforts, make available resource materials, and support new efforts.

John Marks, president of the Common Ground organization searched for persons who could address the strident abortion conflict that on occasion has escalated to murder. Providentially, he was guided to Dr. Adrienne Kaufmann, Order of Saint Benedict. Indeed, she was developing just such a process as her dissertation project at John Mason University. It was this process-method that they used as their initial tool in developing the dialogue in Buffalo. Dr. Kaufmann has graciously granted me permission to write about and quote the spoken information and printed handouts she made available to me. From the outset, the co-director of the Network for Life and Choice was Mary Jacksteit, an attorney and arbitrator. For the first years, they did all the field work together, and then when Dr. Kaufmann had to withdraw for personal reasons, Ms. Jacksteit continued the work.

The way that their process was initiated was this. Persons from both sides of the abortion issue were invited to come for a series of conversations. Publicity made it clear that the purpose was to understand and be understood, not convert and convince.

When persons came together, they were shortly divided into small groups. These groups would include persons of varying views and would remain constant throughout the sessions. However, before the groups met, explanation was given as to what is the Common Ground Process.

They were told that Common Ground is like two interlocking circles. By contrast, when we have a conflict, we usually think of our opponents and us as two quite distant circles—

—and then we shout at each other across the chasm.

By contrast, it is possible to visualize the differing viewpoints as two interlocking circles. The area of intersection represents what the two parties hold in common.

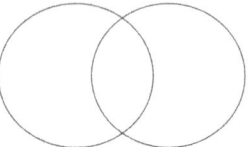

It is much more constructive first to search for the concerns, beliefs, and values that are shared. When we come together on these shared beliefs and values, we are standing on holy ground. From that shared holy ground, we look out and consider the differences.

A common ground process honors each person's piece of the truth. Only God knows it all, but each of us knows something that is of value to the rest.

Further, it is important to recognize a continuum of perspectives. Labels and stereotypes only place people somewhere along a continuum, one side or the other of a line's center. This process will look beyond these. How much wiser it is to refuse to think that one side is a good side and the other side a bad side. There is richness of diversity beyond any labeling.

This builds on the understanding that there are two ways to do critical thinking. One is to look for the weaknesses of the other's viewpoint. The other is connective thinking, which focuses attention on the strengths of the other. It is to search for gems of wisdom within what might indeed be an incomplete text.[2] "In dialogue we ask people to engage in connective thinking—to focus attention on where they agree or resonate with the other's experience and/or beliefs, to listen for the pieces of truth in what is said. Where people place their focus really influences what they hear and remember."[3] Common ground sought for connective thinking.

---

2. "Substantive Dialogue: A Tool for Congregations to Deal with Potentially Divisive Issues Without Becoming Divided," a brief guide prepared by Adrienne Kaufmann and Kate Harvey.

3. http://www.sfcg.org/Programmes/us/us_life.html, 3 of 3.

Then, ground rules, guidelines, and assumptions were presented and explained.

GROUND RULES FOR PARTICIPATION:

1. Respectful speech and behavior toward all present
2. A willingness to understand and be understood, rather than convert and convince
3. Speak for oneself, not as the representative of a group or school of thought
4. Anyone can pass (not speak on a topic) without a negative connotation to passing
5. Confidentiality, meaning no names are ascribed to anything said during the dialogues without that person's express permission to do so.

GUIDELINES FOR PARTICIPATION (The attitudes with which to approach this process):

1. This is DIALOGUE, not debate. We seek light, not heat
2. Each person carries a piece of the truth
3. Genuine curiosity about the other's views is encouraged
4. Struggle is an element of being faithful
5. Compromising one's truth and integrity is unacceptable

ASSUMPTIONS UNDERLYING THE PROCESS:

1. God created and loves each one equally. Each is created in God's image and carries within a spark of the Divine.
2. There is a personal history behind every position, a history that is both whole and broken, a history of the head (what we have been taught) and a history of the heart (what we have experienced).
3. It is God's role to judge others; it is our role to understand them, love them, and work together to create a world more reflective of God's values.
4. Scripture is the Living Word, the primary guide informing our lives.[4]

---

4. Content and discussion of a handout Dr. Kaufmann provided to a gathering of American Baptist Ministers at their biennial in Des Moines, Iowa, June 1999; and Adrienne Kaufmann, "The Common Ground Approach for Leading Dialogue About Divisive Social Issues," personally prepared and circulated by the author.

After this introduction, the small groups were formed. Skills of active listening were taught and practiced. Then each participant was invited to respond to the following question: "What are the personal experiences that have brought you to the place where you now are around the topic we are considering?" This was a process that placed emphasis on personal stories.

Subsequent meetings would continue dialogue operating by the common ground guidelines on topics suggested to each small group and/or selected by the group. Always, all experiences and viewpoints were to be heard with respect and understanding. As Kaufmann has noted, "Dialogue is a gentler, more respectful process than debate. The spirit of dialogue is to acknowledge and honor the humanity of all people present, regardless of their points of view."[5] The conversation might begin with trust-building questions (the first two in the following list) and then go into riskier topics. Here are some of the discussion questions these groups engaged:

- What are the risks and vulnerabilities you feel in being a part of this discussion?
- Who is a hero or heroine for you and why?
- Tell a story related to how your opinion was formed on this issue.
- What is the heart of the issue for you? What is the "bulls eye" around which all other issues circulate?
- How have you been stereotyped, or how have you suffered because of your position?
- If you could put a picture on a magazine cover that expressed the heart of the issue, what would that picture be?
- What do you really believe about when life begins?
- What is your belief about adoption as a response to problem pregnancy?
- What might be done to reduce problem pregnancies?

---

5. Ibid.

- What do you believe is proper protocol for those picketing or demonstrating outside family planning clinics?[6]

As they carried on this conversation, participants noted the insights and strengths they found in each position as well as the weaknesses. The group then discussed both what were the small group's points of agreement as well as their disagreements. After their final session, the group composed a reflection statement that drew together their best wisdom.

In the end, the convening study committee compiled all small group responses and composed them into one reflection piece. This compilation was, in turn, sent to all who took part.[7]

What did leaders hope to gain from this rather demanding process? Not that people move from their original core beliefs. The goals were much more modest, but vitally important. They hoped that persons would come to know and respect others of differing viewpoints; that recognition and understanding of those persons' struggle with the issue would be afforded; and that people were equipped with tools to discuss not only the current dilemma but any difficult issue. And, as the title of the movement indicated, both in relationships and in concepts or actions, a hope was that the groups might find some common ground. When this happened, they succeeded. As one publication described the project intent: "(1) seek to fully understand the others' position and beliefs, and the issue; (2) seek and name the existence of overlapping values, goals, beliefs and important interests (the common ground); and (3) consider ways to act jointly to move forward shared goals."[8] Dr. Kaufmann told me, "I have never had a negative experience carrying on this process. There have been a few isolated individuals who could not participate well and left. But the group experience was always positive and uplifting. There was another miracle—to the best of my knowledge no one ever broke the commitment to confidentiality."

Frederica Matthewes-Green described one such gathering. "... [A] dozen pro-life and pro-choice partisans recently met for the first time in Washington, DC. We discovered that we're not as hardened as the

---

6. Personal conversation with Dr. Kaufmann and Kaufmann, "The Common Ground Approach."

7. *The Common Ground Network for Life and Choice Manual*, that describes these assumptions and processes in detail is available for free download—in both pdf and Word formats—from http://www.sfcg.org/Programmes/us/us_life.html.

8. Ibid.

stereotypes would suggest: One person who had been an activist on his side for 25 years said, 'Any thinking person has to be deeply ambivalent about abortion.' Another introduced herself by saying that she had figured the issue out in black and white, and was afraid that listening to the other side might disrupt her prejudices. She was right, and left the event feeling that she'd made new friends."[9] This essay concluded that each participant, a partisan for a particular point of view, had learned from the others while maintaining the integrity of one's own beliefs.

Sometimes the common concerns that emerge from such a process are more than one might expect. For example, in Buffalo at the conclusion of a dialogue workshop in 1999, the discussion led to a public call for a "New Way" that included seven elements: (1) promoting both male and female sexual responsibility; (2) fostering respect and equality for women; (3) strengthening parent-child communication; (4) reducing the number of teen pregnancies; (5) improving prenatal and maternal care; (6) supporting and funding the choice of adoption; and (7) working together to remove the conditions that lead to abortion.[10]

Matthewes-Green suggested yet another role Common Ground groups could play. "They can simply be a witness." This witness would stand in opposition to the excesses, including violence, of other people who may share their stance on abortion. It might well provide insights to help move toward a society where abortion is less necessary and much less frequent. This witness may call forth a third, a middle and moderate voice in the abortion discussion-debate. She concluded, "Where pro-choice and pro-life people come together to understand each other and discover fragments of agreement, there is hope for clearer skies. A cooler, more temperate breeze may be right around the corner."[11]

For this process to be effective, there are several components that had to be carefully preserved: (a) equal numbers of persons of each position; (b) an impartial facilitator who took no sides, held the group to the ground rules, provided a hearing for all, and moved through the agenda in a timely manner; (c) beginning with story and experience; (d) adhering to the ground rules on dialogue and active listening; (e) connective thinking; (f) a focus on understanding and strengths of each

---

9. Matthewes-Green, "Pro-Life, Pro-Choice: Can We Talk?" 12–13.
10. http://www.nafcm.org/Casepage.html.
11. Matthewes-Green, op. cit.

other's position. "Get it right, hear it well, but you don't have to agree. No one is asked to compromise anything."[12]

The active organization was in existence from 1993 to 2000. The Network extended to twenty communities and was especially active in two cities—Buffalo and Pensacola—where the abortion debate had extended into violence. They designed and carried on community level dialogue, trained facilitators, wrote and developed important literature on this subject, published a newsletter, and linked these efforts together. The formal organization ended in late 1999, due to lack of funding. Some of the stridency of the abortion debate was abating by that time as well.

While the movement came into being to address the abortion controversy, its leaders have been called upon to bring this perspective to other issues that are also dividing the Christian church. Dr. Kaufmann has helped groups seek common ground on such issues as gun control, racial differences, homosexuality, and how to pray. And so, while the specific organization is no longer alive, the creative model as well as training materials to support it is still available. The search for common ground may be even more needed now than it was in the decade when this group facilitated such creative encounters. Co-founder Mary Jacksteit wrote me, "... [T]hank you for describing the work of the Network for Life and Choice. It (really, the people with whom we worked) continues to inspire me in a world where peacemaking can seem a distant vision."[13]

Church Renewal in an Unexpected Place: the Board Meeting

The second parable is about a movement of people that were not directly addressing church conflict—their initial concern was the deadening effect of church board membership and a search for a better way to be church boards.

Charles Olsen was a member of a clergy-discussion group, and it was his turn to present a paper on a subject of his choosing. He had just returned from leading his congregation's annual organizational retreat for the board of elders (the governing board in Presbyterian and Reformed churches). While this was fresh in his mind, he also wondered what was to become of the twelve board members who had just finished their term of service. Too well he recalled what he had heard board

---

12. Kaufmann, personal phone conversation, February 20, 2009.
13. Mary Jacksteit, personal email.

members in his and other churches say at the ends of their terms, "I'm glad it's over ... Whew, I made it ... Never again." Even more, the number of former board members or church officers who became inactive or even dropped out of church dismayed him.

So he wrote and presented his paper on these very real concerns and was amazed at how vigorously his colleagues responded! Clearly he had touched a nerve. And so he set out to learn more and then tell others what he would discover.[14]

Olsen obtained a grant to research church boards, both written material and people's experiences. His interviews revealed "a high level of frustration and even disillusionment among lay people with their experience on church boards, much of it due to a lack of a 'missing' element—spirituality. New members expected that a church-board term would provide an opportunity to develop and deepen their faith. Too often they encountered 'business as usual.'"[15]

The problem is that church boards are usually an imitation of the "creeping board culture" in our society. That is, boards derived their form and method of proceeding from other board cultures operating in their community and in society.

The most prominent of these is the parliamentary culture, using "Robert's Rules of Order." (These guidelines originally came from Henry Marten Robert, a Civil War military engineer, who wrote them to bring some order to the chaotic business meetings at the Baptist church where he was asked to preside. He wrote a basic version of Thomas Jefferson's rules for the United States Congress. They have been expanded and modified many times since.)

While these rules have often helped a conflicted people debate their differences in a reasonably orderly way, they are rules of combat. The church and its boards need to have other ways to make decisions, processes that come from its own self-understanding, guided by scripture.

Other "creeping cultures" also affect how church boards operate, for example, corporate culture. A church board may come to resemble the boards of local corporations in style, method, and purpose. There may be much emphasis on "the bottom line." When a church simply absorbs other board cultures, what happens, as one person put it is that "the

---

14. Olsen, *Transforming Church Boards into Communities of Spiritual Leaders*, ix.
15. Ibid., xi.

church members quit being the church and the pastor quits being the pastor" in that board session.[16]

Leaders in this movement believe that Christian churches are called by God to be guided by the words of Romans 12:2: "Do not be conformed to this world, but be transformed by the renewing of your minds, so that you may discern what is the will of God, what is good and acceptable and perfect." Church board structure and practice should arise out of that transformation of the renewing of our minds. The gospel proclaimed and lived has implications for churches, including how they are led, and how they make decisions.

An ecumenical organization, "Worshipful-Work" was created to find how this might be done and to encourage its widespread use. Ellen Morseth, a member of the Sisters of Charity, BVM, a gifted author and leadership consultant was engaged as a fellow mentor and staff colleague.

This movement's discoveries were that boards seeking both to find the will of God and spiritually enrich board members in this quest need to consider at least four basic practices: (1) history giving and story telling; (2) biblical-theological reflection; (3) prayerful discernment; and (4) "visioning" the future.

The first is history giving and story telling. For a board to function well, it must know the church it serves. Who is this church? What vision inspired its founding, and what visions and missions have animated its life? When did God seem closest? When was the blessing of God upon the church most clearly experienced?

Story telling provides the answers to these questions. Olsen notes, "Whenever community and identity are threatened or lost, the way back is through stories."[17] Key elements of the church's story comprise its DNA, its gene pool.

This story telling must move beyond the typical written church history that often only tells when pastors changed and when buildings were erected. It must move to "thick" history. Who have been the key people that embodied the vision and character of the church? When was this church most alive to its calling and mission? Where has God been at

---

16. Olsen locates seven other board cultures—advisory, political, broker, bureaucratic, managerial, and strategic. For discussion of these see *Transforming Church Boards*, 32–39.

17. Ibid., 55.

work among us since last we met? Through a variety of activities, including shared story telling, a church's unique story—its thick history—can be rediscovered and claimed.

A second practice is biblical-theological reflection. This is not just the responsibility of the pastor—all of us are students of the Bible, all of us inquire into God's ways. We need to do this thoughtful investigation together on behalf of the church.

One way to do biblical-theological reflection is through "story weaving." In this, a group chooses a significant story from the life of the church, unpacks it, and captures its essence, perhaps by choosing a symbol. They may do this by a shared telling of that story. Then the group considers what scripture passages might connect to the story just told. The Bible passage selected is read, or, if well known, also "group told." Then the board explores how to weave the two narratives—our church story and the one from the Bible—together.

In this story weaving, one of at least four outcomes may well happen: (a) the biblical story may bless or affirm the story we told; (b) The biblical story may contradict, confront, stand over against our story and judge it; (c) The biblical story may lure, tease, entice, or invite our story to move toward change; or (d) The biblical story may transform our story into something new.[18]

The third and fourth practices, "prayerful discernment" and "visioning," are closely related. If Christian boards and bodies are to make decisions as servants of God, they must move beyond "majority vote" or "mind of the meeting" to "What is our perception of God's will for us in this matter?"

When this new way of making decisions is begun, the board will need a "discernmentarian" more than a parliamentarian. What is a discernmentarian? This is a person who will be a spiritual guide to the board or group, helping them know where they are in the discernment process.

Discernment is not simply consensus decision making, not a political process, not a logical-rational-ordered-deductive decision making. It is rather a deliberate, prayerful process. This practice is much needed when a board, church, or denomination is facing major, central direction

---

18. Ibid., 70–71. Olsen in turn is utilizing insights from James Hopewell, *Congregations, Stories, and Structures*.

setting decisions. (It is also so demanding and time consuming that a board can engage it for only one, or at most, a few decisions each year.)

Olsen teamed with Danny E. Morris in writing *Discerning God's Will Together*[19] to help groups of people work at discerning God's will for them. They offer ten steps, which are not intended to be automatically and mechanically followed every time. Rather, they are to be used in creative mix as a group seeks divine guidance.

Framing locates the focus for discernment of God's will. The matters to be considered are arranged into a unified whole. The key issue-decision to be faced is clearly stated.

Grounding "jump-starts" the process by seeking the principle that is informed by the values, beliefs, and purposes of the community. If there is no agreement, the discernmentarian might suggest a generic principal such as "God's will: nothing more; nothing less; nothing else."

Shedding involves urging the group to lay aside ego, preconceived notions, false assumptions, biases, and predetermined conclusions so that they can openly consider the matter. In discernment, "indifference" is a positive word meaning that one can let go one's own desire in order to find and do God's will.

Rooting involves searching for biblical references. Also involved is searching Christian heritage, important aspects of the local church's history, gifts from the arts, great hymns of the church that relate to the situation before them.[20]

Listening includes listening to each other, listening for the voices of all affected by the decision, and above all listening for the Spirit of God through and beyond all these other voices.

Exploring is a point where participants are urged to set free their playful imaginations and identify all possible options that lie within the guiding principle. Each option is to be welcomed.

Improving is the process of "bettering" each option until it becomes the best it can possibly be.

Weighing is the time of sorting and testing the options that have emerged. Group members will use all possible sources of wisdom—

---

19. (Bethesda, MD: Alban Institute in arrangement with Upper Room Books, 1997).

20. Ellen Morseth, who was co-leader of Worshipful-Work for a number of years, has written a book with arts and worship resources for each step of discernment. *Ritual and Arts in Spiritual Discernment* (Kansas City, MO: Worshipful-Work, 1999).

symbolic, intuitive, rational, solitude, silence, always seeking to allow God's Spirit to lure persons to that decision where God's Spirit rests

Closing is the time to move toward closure by selecting an option, which the group believes, is in accord with God's leading.

Resting is the final stage where those involved keep the decision near their hearts to detect whether their conclusion primarily brings a sense of consolation, peace, and movement toward God or desolation, distress, and movement away from God.[21]

All of this and more are part of the third practice—prayerful discernment.

The fourth practice, visioning the future, emerges alongside the discernment process. It is both more than and less than a strategic planning process. Rather than detailed plans, it is being open to and searching for God's future for this particular group.

While Worshipful Work was not primarily designed to help deal with conflicts, it has served churches, organizations and denominations in that way. Groups using the Worshipful-Work model have effectively addressed impasses on building decisions, differing views of worship, dilemmas over the use of a huge windfall for a church—these and many other potentially divisive issues. They have played a vital part in both the healing and the renewal of many churches and ecclesiastical organizations.

Since their center was formally launched in 1995 (this was following a four year period of investigation and discovery), staff mentors of Worshipful-Work have introduced this model to some 35,000 people and have distributed 35,000–40,000 copies of their books, manuals, handbooks surveys and videotapes. Churches, regional organizations and whole denominations have made this a way of life for their governance and decision making.

However, this creative movement has also experienced a changed circumstance. Charles Olsen, the founding director retired in 2000. After 9/11 in 2001, conferencing and fund raising declined precipitously. Worshipful-Work's governing board (called the Board of Discerning Overseers) found it necessary to dismiss its remaining staff and sell its property.

---

21. This has been a brief overview and summary of chapter 4 (pages 65–93) of *Discerning God's Will Together*.

After a long period of reflection, and discernment, in 2007, this board concluded it was led to dissolve Worshipful-Work as a resourcing and programming organization. Fortunately, they were in touch with an entity that was carrying on some of its mission. They entrusted the trademark and the task of training persons in the discernment process to Water in the Desert Ministries, located in Albuquerque, New Mexico.

This ministry is staffed by two persons with intimate knowledge and involvement for many years with the Worshipful-Work organization. Judith Todd was involved in the movement from its early discoveries. Val Isenhower had served as Coordinator of Ministry for Worshipful Work. Persons desiring to receive guidance in these distinct ways of board discernment and spiritual enrichment of board work should now contact Water in the Desert Ministries.[22] Some of the earlier literature, new works on discernment, and workshops-retreats are available from this source.

Plowshares Institute: Widespread Empowerment of Peace Builders

In the early 1980s, when Robert and Alice Frazer Evans, missionaries with a specialty in conflict management, were expelled from Uganda, they were invited to take up a work of reconciliation and training by Bishop Desmond Tutu in South Africa. There, they joined forces with Ronald Kraybill and others. Together, they developed their skills and techniques as they trained hundreds of community leaders to be agents of conflict transformation in the widespread tension and community unrest that country was experiencing.

Strengthened and encouraged by the vital impact of their ministry there, they have trained and consulted with their intercultural perspective around the world and in many U.S. trouble spots. Plowshares Institute was founded in 1981 to address issues of injustice through education, research, and service.

Their eclectic approach is, in many ways, similar to the methods of others. At the same time, their widespread international experience, their inter-cultural and interfaith perspective, and their personal genius and energy give their work a unique and special emphasis. Further, they

---

22. http://waterinthedesert.org/news-and-information/worshipful-work.html.

have designed manuals so that those who experience the training can in turn pass the wisdom and skills on to others.[23]

In contrast to those who seek conflict management, or conflict resolution, or even conflict prevention (as we discussed in chapter three), they prefer "conflict transformation." "Transformation asserts the belief that conflict can be a catalyst for deep-rooted, enduring, positive change in individuals, relationships, and structures."[24] As noted in chapter two, this has at least two aspects: persons experience *empowerment* when their value, uniqueness, needs, thoughts are recognized and honored; and they experience *recognition* when they see the corresponding value, needs, and dignity of others.

While there are many roles a peace builder can play, they encourage that of mediator. A mediator is one who does not provide or enforce a solution, but rather helps the conflicted parties through a process where they discover, agree, and implement their own solution. This often—not always—is a most helpful role in aiding conflicted parties to a solution with lasting effect.

The Evans's and Kraybill suggest that it is important to know the exact nature (and sources) of a conflict, and that it usually arises from one or more of the following matters:

- *Resources*—such as land, money, or objects.

- *Information*—for example, what is the true and accurate information about this situation?

- *Values*—which include what persons hold dear from faith, personal experience, and culture. They note that because conflicts here may feel like a threat to one's identity, these are often the most difficult to resolve—and this is the specific area on which we are concentrating in this volume.

- *Interests or needs*—such important and powerful human needs such as identity, respect, or participation, among others.

---

23. Their two manuals are *Peace Skills: Manual for Community Mediators* by Ronald S. Kraybill with Robert A. Evans and Alice Frazer Evans. In the following discussion, this will be called "Kraybill" in references; and *Peace Skills: Leader's Guide* by Alice Frazer Evans and Robert A. Evans with Ronald S. Kraybill,) called "Evans" in the following discussion.

24. Kraybill, op. cit., 5.

- *Relationships*—including people's past history, misunderstandings, hurts, family involvements, and more.
- *Structures*—social, governmental, economic, organizational structures often impact who has access to power and privilege.

Of course, more than one of these is almost always a part of any conflict. These varied causes of conflict can be remembered by use of the acrostic *RIVIRS*.[25]

When a conflict arises, there needs to be a process of "pre-mediation." The key players in the conflict are identified. Each is visited personally with an invitation to sit down in a face to face meeting to explore the concern under contention. Each is given promises of safety, respect, and a chance to tell one's story with a goal of seeing if some understandings can be reached.

If conflicting parties agree, the mediator calls them together, outlines and guides them in a four stage process (which may take one or several sessions).

Stage one is "Introduction." At this point, the mediator's main task is providing safety. S/he convenes them in a safe and neutral place, arranges the room in an egalitarian manner, welcomes all, states goals, offers ground rules (not interrupting, confidentiality, respect) and gains commitment to these. There is also agreement as to how much time will be spent in the current session.

Stage two is "Storytelling." Offering understanding is the mediator's central focus. The mediator invites party A and then party B to tell their story without interruption—their perspective on the situation. It is important to show respect, to listen carefully, to communicate understanding through paraphrasing and summary. As the mediator offers the same attentive listening to each party, s/he listens for common ground between them, as well as for issues, for needs and feelings.

The third stage is "Problem Solving." The mediator seeks to build ownership. At this point the mediator states out loud the common concerns and common ground that aggrieved parties share; also stated are the issues that need addressing. The mediator seeks agreement about the issues needing attention. They then turn to working on the issues one at a time (perhaps starting with the easiest to resolve). Moving away from demands and focusing on the persons' interests, and needs, they

25. Ibid., 14–16.

generate options. This may be done by brainstorming possible solutions. The options are evaluated by all concerned; the most fitting selected; and implementation planned.

Stage four is "Agreement"—a most important stage of the hard work of negotiation to this point is to be fruitfully maintained. Together, mediator and the conflicted parties summarize the agreements made, being as clear and simple as possible. They also need to take care that the specifics of who, what, when, where, and how are addressed. The mediator needs also to assure that the settlement is just and contributes to the dignity of each. There needs to be provision for follow-up, for evaluation on how the agreed process is going, and for settling other conflicts that might arise. And there also needs to be a way—that fits both participants and their cultures—to seal this agreement. Perhaps, this will be a written and signed agreement, a handshake, a meal, a prayer, a blessing, or some other ritual.[26]

Conflict is messy and multi-layered. Of course, mediation is not as neat and orderly as described in the previous paragraphs. The Plowshare people have demonstrated, however, that caring community leaders can be trained and empowered with this road map and the skills to help people follow it. Conflict need not simmer or break out into violence. Peace can be built. Recognition and empowerment can occur, and reconciliation does happen.

Plowshare's strategy of conflict transformation is a message with an eager audience. They have been invited and offered conflict transformation training projects in East Timor, Hong Kong, Indonesia, Kenya, Uganda, Zimbabwe, Union of South Africa, and in many cities in North America. People using their gifts have addressed conflicts in neighborhoods, between friends, in housing projects, between work-mates, between military bases and the communities they were leaving, between city officials and disaffected citizens, and among church people. The need continues and grows, and the story goes on.

Conclusion

Parables stand on their own. A good storyteller lets the listener or reader draw one's own conclusions. You are free to do that. At the same time,

---

26. This process is summarized in Kraybill on page 28, and described in more detail on pages 25–82. A workshop to train persons how to be mediators is provided in detail in Evans, 43–79. Plowshares' web site is www.plowsharesinstitute.com.

I reflect on what I have learned from these groups that I explored and then described for you.

I learned that revolution can start from the middle. Those who began talking with each other in the Common Ground movement knew they did not agree with each other, but neither did they agree at all points with many of those who believed as they did. And so they created a new force in the discussion—a growing group in the middle who discovered more, achieved more, and brought sanity and respect to a harsh conflict. Thus, these courageous persons in the middle (who never gave up their personal convictions) achieved more than anyone might have thought possible.

I learn that value conflicts are the most difficult of all conflicts, and we Christian folk are in the midst of a number of value conflicts. I also learn that most conflicts have a variety of factors within them, and I am made more sensitive to all of those aspects.

I learn that growth and transformation are possible in conflicts and begin to develop the concepts and skills to help this happen more often.

I discover that prayerful discernment seeking God's will for the church may not only lead to wise decisions, it might bypass and overcome conflicts that would usually occur.

Some of the ways of claiming the gifts and transforming possibilities in conflict are beginning to emerge.

QUESTIONS AND ACTIVITIES FOR GROUP REFLECTION

1. As you think of a conflict in your life, what wisdom, insights, or skills did persons in these parables offer that might be helpful?

2. Which of these parables, if any, personally interests you the most?

3. Is there one of the groups or individuals described in these three parables that you would like to research more and report to the group? About which of these, if any, would you like more information, and possibly training?

4. Are you aware of other groups that are working at some sort of peace building activity that would be worthy candidates to be mentioned in a chapter like this? If so, what are they and what is their mission?

5. As regards conflict, what parables of hope and promise do you have to tell?

8

Insights from Studies of Persons and Communities

... We may also gain from the thoughts of contemporary leaders. Studies of how people interact as individuals and in communities provide food for thinking, acting, and relating ...

FOR YOUR PERSONAL OR GROUP WORSHIP

Scripture

For just as the body is one and has many members, and all the members of the body, though many, are one body, so it is with Christ. For in the one Spirit we were all baptized into one body—Jews or Greeks, slaves or free—and we were all made to drink of one Spirit ...

Indeed, the body does not consist of one member but of many. If the foot would say, "Because I am not a hand, I do not belong to the body," that would not make it any less a part of the body... As it is, there are many members but one body. The eye cannot say to the hand "I have no need of you," nor again the head to the feet, "I have no need of you." ... If one member suffers, all suffer together with it; if one member is honored, all rejoice together with it....

Now you are the body of Christ and individually members of it. (1 Cor 12:12–14, 20–21, and 26–27)

A Word to Ponder

As long as we are on earth, the love that unites us will bring us suffering by our very contact with one another, because this love is the resetting of a Body of broken bones. Even saints cannot live with saints on this earth without some anguish, without some pain at the differences that come between them.

There are two things [people] can do about the pain of disunion with other [people]. They can love or they can hate. (Thomas Merton)[1]

FOR YOUR THOUGHT AND REFLECTION

Some of the nation's top psychiatrists are now advocating the creation of a new category of mental illness. If approved, it will be included in diagnostic manuals. This new malady would be called "Relational Disorders" and would be applied, not to *individuals* as psychiatric diagnoses always have done, but to *groups*. Initially, attention would be directed to couples, siblings, and families.

These mental health specialists note that some people are healthy except when it comes to certain relationships. If this new diagnosis is accepted, couples who constantly quarrel or parents and children who clash could be diagnosed with mental illness and treated, perhaps even with drugs. Not all agree with this approach, however. There is also debate as to whether such relational maladies are medical ailments or social problems.[2]

For us in churches, a notion of relational disorders stirs a nod of recognition. Some of us, who function quite well in other settings, somehow do not do so well when issues arise either at our church or between churches.

This brings us to those who study human interactions—both those of individuals and of communities. What help is there from the wisdom gained from studies of individuals and communities to aid this search for better understandings and ways in our conflicts?

I will offer you some insights from a wide variety of pastoral theologians and behavioral scientists. These will offer perspective on why some conflicts are so hard to deal with. There are also suggestions for some ways to be helpful in spite of the difficulties.

---

1. Thomas Merton, *New Seeds of Contemplation*, 72, as found in Arthur Paul Boers, *Never Call Them Jerks: Healthy Responses to Difficult Behavior*, 26.
2. This article was contained in the *Kansas City Star*, September 1, 2002, A12.

Perspective from Systems Concepts and Strategies

First, consider that we are an inter-related system. Therefore, there is more to a conflict than might first appear, and there are varieties of ways to respond.

An important theory about the human condition anticipates the idea of "relational disorders." In modern form, it has been around for fifty years or more. I speak of family systems theory. In this theory, the focus is on the family (or other group) and its many interactions as an inter-related system, rather than on the individual.

When one person in a family has problems—for example, poor school performance, running away, or drug or alcohol abuse—systems therapists look not so much at the individual as at the family process and tensions. They may see the acting out person as the "identified patient" of some tension, some problem, or some other malfunction that needs to be addressed within the whole family. Change in the family can bring about change in the individual, and change in any individual affects the family in turn.

If this inter-related behavior and feeling is true in families, it is equally true in churches. As a matter of fact, it is extremely helpful it is to think of churches this way. As with families, it is important to recognize the connections between people. We can understand people only within the context of their relationships. No one of us lives or acts in isolation. Indeed, we are all affected by each other's behavior.

Ronald Richardson notes, "Change in one member in a congregation can affect the whole. Most often the change in that one member has been preceded by changes in others. The system is the total of all the members and their different actions and reactions."[3]

As Charles Cosgrove and Dennis Hatfield helpfully write, "The local church is a large familylike system made up of many smaller familylike subsystems."[4] They might have added that the church is also made up of families of families—multi-generation families whether all the generations are present or not.

Indeed, in his classic work on this subject, Edwin Friedman examines in detail the relationship between the family systems of members in

---

3. Ronald Richardson, *Creating a Healthier Church: Family Systems Theory, Leadership, and Congregational Life*, 25, 28.

4. Charles Cosgrove and Dennis Hatfield, *Church Conflict: The Hidden Systems Behind the Fights*, 19.

the congregation, the congregation as a family system, and the clergy's family. He convincingly points out that all of these are interrelated in multiple ways, a truth clergy can utilize for self-awareness, effective ministry, and congregational functioning.[5] It also helps one understand some otherwise inexplicable church conflicts.

Actually, the church is not just one system, but rather many systems. Within a church there are cultural systems, structural systems (how are we officially organized and who is authorized to make the decisions), communication systems, and economic systems. We are focusing mostly on the emotional-relational system, although this system is affected by and affects all the other systems.

The New Testament anticipates a system way of thinking when it compares the church to a human body. In Rom 12:4–5, we read: "For as in one body we have many members and not all the members have the same function, so we, who are many, are one body in Christ, and individually we are members one of another." In 1 Cor 12, the implications are elaborated. Verse 21 states: "The eye cannot say to the hand, 'I have no need of you' nor again the head to the feet, 'I have no need of you.'" And again verse 26 states: "If one member suffers, all suffer together with it; if one member is honored, all rejoice together with it."

While we may know these verses well, we may not have noticed the wisdom about conflict that this metaphor of body contains. When I hit my thumb with a hammer, I don't isolate that feeling to the thumb. My whole body reacts, is in pain, is "out of whack," and responds crabbily to anyone standing close at the time! That same dynamic may be going on in church conflicts. Pain tends to get distributed.

Other metaphors also help us understand the church as a system. We may compare the church to a delicately balanced mobile. Touch any one part of it, even slightly, and the whole thing shivers, trembles, and re-adjusts.

Or we may compare it to an exercise youth groups used to do. We would all lie down on the floor, each one's head on some one else's stomach. Supposedly we would just lie there. However, any reaction—a giggle, a hiccup, a feeling of tenseness or distress in any one of us would quickly pass through all of us.

---

5. See Edwin Friedman, *Generation to Generation: Family Process in Church and Synagogue*.

Each of these metaphors gives us some indication of how to understand church as a family system of families and family like groups (such as choirs, boards, Sunday School classes, etc.). We need also to note that in the New Testament, Paul uses the body image both for one local church and for the wider church, the church universal.

There is much more to know about churches as systems.[6] This brief summary provides some clues as to possible causes of puzzling conflicts. It also offers more helpful ways to respond. Here are some of those possibilities:

a) A system may have unspoken but binding rules for how it operates, and these laws may be operating when a conflict occurs. (For example, though we profess to want new members, no authoritative leadership may be granted to them.)

b) A system may have long term habits for dealing with conflict that come into play. For example, Speed Leas and Paul Kittlaus tell of a church where the minister moved the pews from parallel to the communion table to angles with it and around it. After that, attendance went down, members withdrew, and the church disintegrated. From the outside, this would seem a simple conflict to solve—talk about it, and if people don't like the new arrangement, put the pews back. However the congregation's habitual avoiding of conflict (and probably some accumulated resentments) hampered such a response.[7]

c) Emotional climates within a church or in the world around it may stir emotional-conflictual responses to issues that had long lay dormant. It is a well known fact that the same congregation may respond differently to similar crises at different times, say an ineffective staff member, or a moral lapse in a church leader. The reason for the differences in response likely has to do with what else is affecting the emotional life and tone of the congregation at the time. A worthy question to ask when any conflict

---

6. In addition to the previous three books listed, see Arthur Paul Boers, *Never Call Them Jerks: Healthy Responses to Difficult Behavior* and Peter L. Steinke, *Healthy Congregations: A Systems Approach.*

7. See Speed Leas and Paul Kittlaus, *Church Fights: Managing Conflict in the Local Church* for a discussion of fear, withdrawal, and nonparticipation as a part of church conflicts, 109–13.

arises is not only what the issue is, but why this is happening with this deeper level of intensity now.

d) The conflict may be more over process than content, the how rather than the what. The dissonance may be over inequities of power and decision-making authority, or how concerns are heard and responded to. It maybe a resurfacing of old grudges or a re-stirring of previous tensions. A key question to explore is how does our system work? Are there adjustments we can make to the system that correct the pain that some members are feeling in it? Is there healing of memories that is needed?

e) Attention needs to be given to the many interlocking triangles. The concept of triangulation is an important one in family systems theory. Friedman notes, "An emotional triangle is formed by any three persons or issues." He adds, "The basic law of emotional triangles is that when any two parts of a system become uncomfortable with one another, they will 'triangle in' or focus on a third person, or issue, as a way of stabilizing their own relationship with one another."[8]

A triangle is thus a relationship in which two people communicate through a third party (which may be a person or an issue). The more problematic the relationship, the more intense will be the focus on the third corner of the triangle. And so, the stated reason for the conflict may be the "identified issue," that is the point at which two parties (groups or individuals) have concentrated because of their discomfort with each other. The "identified issue" may be a symptom of other problems, and it may not be the most significant issue in and of itself. One may need to look for strategies to explore the tension between the two parties before any progress can be made on the issue on which they have focused.

Those are but a few examples in which church/family systems theory brings insight to our conflicts with each other. Not only are the conflicts more complex than we often think, there are infinitely more ways to understand the conflict and strategies to be of assistance when conflict occurs.

Even though church systems are a complex and complicated mystery, systems knowledge can be used to provide a clearer path through

---

8. Friedman, op. cit., 35.

conflict than might otherwise happen. Duane L. Ruth-Heffelbower and Alice Price advise that the systems-wise leaders will pay close attention to: 1. interpersonal relationships; 2. communication/information sharing; 3. decision making; and 4. leadership. Here is their preliminary guidance for progressing in conflict within a congregational system:

- The right group must be given the appropriate amount of authority to develop an action plan.
- The congregation must be kept informed at the appropriate level and must be invited to provide feedback to the planning group
- Final agreement on the plan of action must occur before the plan is carried out.
- Implementation must be under the supervision of the person or persons to whom the congregation entrusts such responsibility.
- Even after the activity begins, ongoing interactive feedback is important between leaders and followers.[9]

While the mysteries of systems are never entirely predictable, these common sense steps may help one traverse the terrain with as little pain as possible for all concerned.

Awareness of Crippling Structure and Bureaucracy

Second, be aware that one specific and troubling aspect of church life may be its structure. This may be particularly true for traditional, aging churches with declining membership. Quite possibly in such congregations, the organizational structure may overwhelm member volunteer resources. Further, this structure-bureaucracy may stifle or confuse purposeful decision making. Douglas Bixby writes of this eloquently, terming it the "church monster."

> The church monster is the extensive conflict, anxiety, and bureaucracy that grows out of poor structure and the inability to make decisions effectively and efficiently. What was once a church mouse, a small irritating pest, is now a church monster—a huge, devastating problem. Churches are having a hard time surviving, let alone thriving, in the midst of all this conflict and anxiety.

---

9. Duane Ruth-Heffelblower and Alice Price, "Systems Failures and How to Correct Them," in Marlin E. Thomas (ed.) *Transforming Conflict in Your Church*, 38.

And the overgrown, complicated church structures we have developed in the past not only feed into this, they also keep our churches from establishing the kind of momentum they need to survive and thrive in the present age.[10]

Of course, addressing this very real problem may stir even more conflict, including battles over revision of constitution and by-laws. Bixby suggests a common sense approach: offer a reasonable plan for participative decision making on all major questions facing the church. Next, move to suspend the church constitution and structure for one year and try the new simplified plan. Then, from a different place in their history, a congregation can choose how it wants to do its planning and decision making. Bixby is convinced that the future church must have less structure than most do these days, but the church will still need some. Fitting structure and decision making policies for today and tomorrow's over-busy and over-committed church people require discernment. I highly commend his book as a guide as to this can be done—and how some congregations have done so.

He proposes—and demonstrates—a democratic, parliamentary and straightforward process of gathering all the information, deciding and moving forward. His model is a simplification of church's usual ways of doing these things. As such it is a different approach than the "Worshipful Work" model, described in chapter seven, but both address similar problems. These two strategies offer varying ways to address a source not only of frequent conflict, but of frustration and disillusion with the church—the overly organized or poorly organized congregation or church board.

The Delicacy of Values-Beliefs Conflicts

Now, our focus changes. I have been discussing community complexities and now turn to a personal-individual one. It is this—the difficulty and pain some issues stir in me or you.

Third, be aware that conflicts over values and beliefs are particularly painful and difficult. We Christians need to be patient when dealing with many of our issues, because values and beliefs are so much a part of

---

10. Douglas J. Bixby, *Challenging the Church Monster: From Conflict to Community,* 15.

us. When someone questions or criticizes my personally held beliefs or values, it feels like an attack on me. That is a devastating experience.

Where do these personal beliefs-values come from? They have been absorbed and claimed from a lifelong journey of faith and other treasured experiences. Persons we admired and who influenced us have contributed. We have internalized the beliefs such persons expressed and made them our own. They feel like part of who we are. Bible study groups, worship, conversation with friends, historical events, the culture of community-region-nation, and more have confirmed and strengthened our concepts of right and wrong and the issues where they should be applied.

Then, along comes a conflict that challenges cherished beliefs-values, a conflict in which the other side appears to have at least a smidgen of truth. What do I do? I may panic and/or resist. I may withdraw and refuse to talk about it. Indeed, it may seem that my whole world is under attack, trembling and shaking. For a time, I lack any constructive way to deal with this conflict. These are understandable responses.

As I ponder this response, I am helped to understand by considering Leas and Kittlaus's description of three types of conflict. There is *intrapersonal conflict*, the conflicts one has within oneself when different beliefs, decisions, conclusions seem to collide with one another. Then there is *interpersonal conflict* where two people or groups of people feel incompatible with each other. And there is *substantive conflict*, which is about the content of issues. Substantive conflicts can be over information-facts, means-methods, goals, and values.[11]

These authors put conflicts over beliefs-values in the last category. However, as I see it, a value conflict involves all three of these at the same time. My inner world of meaning and belief is being challenged and upset with perplexing alternatives. I am also called upon to deal with people different from me. Further, there is considerable difference about how I see what information and views are valid and what is the proper response to this issue. Often the conflict is about a subject I would rather ignore or avoid. All of this is tied up to my personal identity as a believing-acting self. And it hurts—a value conflict is painful indeed.

If it is that difficult, how do we ever overcome the barriers and begin to work on these types of conflicts with each other? We might begin by recognizing all of this and acknowledging the mutual pain.

---

11. Leas and Kittlaus, op.cit., 29–34.

Insights from Studies of Persons and Communities 123

Then, perhaps, we can proceed by being very gentle with each other. I recall what one of my counseling supervisors used to advise me. He said, "Respect your counseling client's resistance." Then he would continue, "But push on that resistance."

Quite likely, that is what we need to do with each other—respect the other's values, but push on them a little. Also, we need to recognize when we have been pushed enough for a while.

While not written specifically about conflicts of beliefs or values, David Augsburger's statement on how to do "Carefronting" may be helpful. He suggests a conversation something like this.

> I care about our relationship. I feel deeply about the issue at stake.
> I want to hear your view. I want to clearly express mine.
> I want to respect your insights. I want respect for mine.
> I trust you to be able to handle my honest feelings [and beliefs and values]. I want you to trust me with yours.
> I promise to stay with the discussion until we've reached an understanding [or, perhaps, as much understanding as we can achieve]. I want you to keep working with me until we've reached a new understanding.
> I will not trick, pressure, manipulate, or distort the differences. I want your unpressured, clear, honest view of our differences.
> I give you my loving, honest respect. I want your caring-confronting response.[12]

I believe it is possible to do this in spite of the difficulties. The story of the women in "The Search for Common Ground" from the previous chapter is an example of people doing this, and it gives me hope. I urge you to read it again in the light of this discussion.

Insights About Stages and Levels of Conflict

Again, our focus changes, now to the varieties of conflict itself. Fourth, be aware that conflicts have stages and levels that can inform us.

When I am drawn into a conflict, it is good to ask, "What kind of struggle is this?" I need to ask not only is this conflict what it appears and what values are at stake, but I also need to be aware of where we are in this conflict? How long has it been brewing, and how long has it been active? How intense is it, and what if any damage has already been

---

12. David W. Augsburger, *The Love Fight: Caring Enough to Confront,* 5.

done? And, how does knowing all this impact how I conduct myself in the conflict before me?

In his book, *Moving Your Church Through Conflict*, Speed Leas identifies preliminary warning signs and then five levels of church conflict. I will summarize his findings and reflect on the ways it helps to answer these questions.

He first reminds us that there are many early warning signs of conflict. For one thing, there may be environmental factors that increase a congregation's susceptibility to conflict. Economic recessions, a shrinking population from which to draw members, declining church membership, the emergence of a nearby "super, full service church" with which unfavorable comparisons can be made, the departure of a long term pastor or the arrival of a new one—all of these may contribute to a conflict prone environment.

In addition, there may also be specific behaviors within the congregation that are early indicators. Rumors or complaints—loud and straightforward or timid and anonymous may be such an indication. So are declines in participation, attendance, or giving. Changes in lay leadership (including resignations) may also indicate or contribute to conflict. These and many others may imply that there is discontent that needs prompt and early attention.[13]

Then, Leas identifies five levels of conflict given in order of ascending difficulty. He titles Level I "Problems to Solve." There is a real conflict here that needs addressing. At this level, the objective is "to fix the problem, to use rational methods to determine what is wrong."

Contending persons believe collaborative methods are possible. They will engage in the conflict openly with complete disclosure of relevant information. Language is "clear, specific, oriented to the here and now, not loaded with innuendo."

Level II is "Disagreement." Here, a new concern enters—self-protection, not getting hurt, looking good. This may take over as the major objective. There is more shrewdness and calculation, lining up sides, and gaining allies.

The language shifts from specific to general. "People are saying ... Some folks I know ... We need more openness." People are more distrustful and are cautious about sharing all they know. Hostile put-down humor may enter in.

---

13. Speed B. Leas, *Moving Your Church Through Conflict*, 13–15.

Level III is "Contest." A "win/lose" feeling comes in on this level. The objective of contending parties has switched from self-protection to winning. By now, it is "win at any cost."

Both in language and in the way parties see things, distortion creeps in, and this in a variety of ways. I may see myself as much better than I am and you as much worse. I may dichotomize, that is choose to see everything in neat, dual packages, right or wrong, stay or leave, fight or flee.

There are no shades of meaning or combinations of possibilities in this thinking. I may generalize in an out of control way, "You always . . . never . . . Everybody." I may fall prey to assumptions that not only can I read your mind, I know your motives. (And, your mind and your motives are not good.)

Level IV is "Fight/Flight." Now, beyond wanting to win, the parties want to hurt and/or get rid of those on the other side. Neither side believes the other side can or will change. Rather than the good of the whole organization, it is the good of the subgroup of which I am a part that has leaped to the highest priority. Primeval instincts of survival under fear of attack come to the fore.

There is even less talking with those on the other side. When there is talk, it is of principles and rights—such as truth, freedom, and justice—which my side has and your side lacks. There is also inability to distinguish between persons and the ideas imputed to them.

Level V is "Intractable Situations." Conflict is beyond the control of the contending parties; it is "conflict run amok." Objectives have moved on from "merely" removing or punishing the opposition to destroying it.

Leas writes, "At Level V parties usually perceive themselves as part of an eternal cause, fighting for universal principles. Since the ends are all-important, they believe they are compelled to continue to fight; they cannot stop. Indeed, the costs to society, truth, and God of withdrawal from the fight are perceived as greater than the costs of defeating the others even through prolonged conflict. Therefore, continuing the fight is the only choice; one cannot choose to stop fighting."[14]

There is much we can learn from Leas's careful analysis. One thing is that we do well to be sensitive to signs of conflict and offer as many

---

14. Ibid., 22. The preceding is a summary of pages 19–22 with occasional indicated quotes.

early responses and interventions as possible. While we admitted earlier that conflict prevention is neither possible nor always desirable, conflict awareness is always an important skill. Hearing concerns and differences as early as possible on as small a scale as possible is wise and prudent. If I am one of the parties in the conflict, working on solutions early is also wise.

Another insight is that different levels of conflict need different skills to be helpful to the parties involved. For example, at Level I, "Problems to Solve," straightforward dialogue may suffice. At Level II, "Disagreement," there will need to be considerable effort to help both sides to feel safe and to have opportunity both to tell their story and hear the other's.

At Level III, "Contest," there may need to give much attention to common goals, common history, and common values. The leader will need to help participants on each side clarify their interests and look for common ground. Attention may also need to be given to the difference between assumptions and reality.

At Level IV "Fight/Flight," perhaps more formal parliamentary methods may be needed. This may include arbitration and group votes where consensus cannot be gained. There may need to be emphasis on rules and fair play. At Level V, "Intractable Situations," the parties may need to be kept apart. Perhaps only a "go between" carrying messages and offers can effect any contact at all.

Yet another insight is that not all of us in a conflict may be at the same level at the same time. The "us" may be an individual, a family, a congregation, a denomination, or a movement within the wider church. And, those within the "us" may need to talk to each other about the differences among "us" as well as converse with those who are not "us".

There may be strong partisans urging us on to levels III, IV, and V. And there may be others of us—possibly many of us—who believe an issue needs attention but want to confront it on a level I or II. We may then find ourselves in a worthy but uncomfortable and lonely position—we oppose the stridency of some with whom we agree, and we oppose others on the basis of belief and conviction. We are the people in the middle of which we spoke earlier—the people from whom a revolution in how we deal with each other can begin.

One place of healing for a polarized church may be just such a "revolution from the middle." Persons on both sides of divisive issues can refuse to follow their leaders into more destructive conflict. Rather, they can choose to carry on constructive, respectful, but non-compromising dialogue with other Christians with whom they disagree on this issue.

I also refer you to a recent work that builds on and elaborates Leas's perspective. George W. Bullard, Jr., in his book, *Every Congregation Needs a Little Conflict*, explores seven intensity levels in church conflict (rather than five) and the fitting strategies helping a church deal with conflict on each of those levels. He also heads an organization that provides extensive training in applying these insights.[15]

Personal Involvement and Perspective

Before concluding our brief survey of insights from social scientists and pastoral theologians, we touch on one more matter. It is this: conflict affects each one of us personally. We cannot approach a disagreement entirely objectively or dispassionately. Therefore, we need to consider our response to our own emotions even as we attempt to help others in the conflict deal with theirs.

Fifth, I am wise to face each conflict personally involved but open; I need to be fused a little, but differentiated more. For all our knowledge and information about conflict, when an argument actually comes, it does strange things to us. In order to be effective, either as participants or as mediators, we need to be aware of this impact. And then, as much as possible, we need to choose the stance we will adopt when in the midst of conflict.

There are two closely related aspects of this. One has to do with my personal stake in any conflict. I need to be clearly aware of my personal motives. The better I know my own motives and interests, the more honest I will be in this conflict. In this connection, Lewis Coser has noted, "Conflicts in which the participants feel that they are . . . fighting not for self but only for the ideals of the groups . . . are likely to be more radical and merciless than those that are fought for personal reasons. Elimination of the personal element tends to make conflict sharper in the absence of modifying elements which personal factors would normally introduce."[16] Awareness of my own intense personal interest and that of the other humanizes and softens the sharp edges of conflict, at least a little bit. That's one aspect.

15. See George W. Bullard, Jr. *Every Congregation Needs a Little Conflict*.
16. Leas and Kitlaus, op. cit., 44. They are quoting Lewis Coser, *The Functions of Social Conflict*, 118.

But there is another—it is how my feelings and thoughts intersect and influence me in a conflict. Often the terms "fused" and "differentiated" are used to describe this. How do I relate feelings and thoughts, togetherness and separateness? Are my feelings the same as my thoughts (fused), or can I separate feelings from thoughts, and sometimes act on my best thoughts (differentiated)? Do I feel totally connected to you with both of us responsible for the other's feelings and actions (fused) or do I perceive the distance and difference between us (differentiated)?

All of us are fused at times—with family members, with church, with friends. A congregation that is mostly fused confuses feelings and facts and has a hard time sorting out responsibility and accountability. In the wise ordering of family or congregational life, a healthy amount of differentiation is needed.

In a congregation with high differentiation, there will be more persons speaking and owning their own positions, values, and beliefs. These persons will be able to consider options and choices, anticipating the consequences of each direction. They will perceive a situation more accurately and may well have the flexibility to respond. Further, the church may be more able to identify and achieve common goals, and to maintain connections with each other in spite of differences.

Differentiated leaders understand that their primary responsibility is taking charge of oneself. They can then be freer to help others decide, rather than attempting to change, motivate, or move others from their original stances. That means part of being a differentiated leader is not becoming over involved or over anxious over the emotions others may direct at one. Edwin Friedman frequently commented on how helpful is the "nonanxious presence." This makes sense, because as we earlier noted, the fears and anxieties of people distort their perceptions and impair their thinking. A calm leader with a sense of ownership of one's perspective on the issue and also a sense of where one's responsibility begins and ends can in turn calm upset members and help them think more accurately and constructively.

Speed Leas recalls a time when such a presence was most reassuring to him. A jet plane on which he was a passenger lost its hydraulic system in the air, leaving the plane without brakes, without the mechanism to lower the landing gear, and without the use of regular controls for steering the plane. The pilot came on the intercom and explained the situation. Then he also explained what he was going to do and described his training to deal with just such situations. Though unusual, he assured them that he and his crew could handle this quite readily. That nonanxious presence gained the passengers' confidence in him. They in turn remained calm, while the pilot did as he promised.[17]

In this chapter we have enriched our perspective by naming and summarizing some important wisdom about why individuals and communities behave the way we do. Perhaps this can call forth a greater understanding and patience with others and with ourselves. This information also suggests skills and sensitivity that all who would help the church heal need to pursue. It encourages a healthy dose of listening, of respect for that which we do not yet know, of humility.

I hope this little survey increases our awareness about how complex conflicts may be and invites us to greater sensitivity and skillfulness in working through our own and others' conflicts. Then we may be like that pilot, who not only calmed the passengers but landed them safely.

QUESTIONS AND ACTIVITIES FOR GROUP REFLECTION

1. Have you ever been a part of a conflict, which took directions that you did not understand? If so, would you tell about it? Are there any clues in this chapter for understanding the puzzling directions of that conflict?

2. What do you find most helpful about family systems theory in understanding conflict? Where are you unconvinced or puzzled?

3. What values conflicts can you discuss-debate objectively? Which ones stir deep feelings in you? Do you understand why the difference? What does this imply for how you conduct these respective discussions?

4. As you consider Speed Leas's concept of five levels of conflict, which levels have you experienced? What about each conflict caused you to identify it with a specific level?

5. As regards your family are you mostly fused or differentiated? As regards your church family, are you mostly fused or differentiated? What leads you to answer as you do?

---

17. Cited in Boers, 104–105, from *Leadership and Conflict*, 61–62.

6. Have you ever been helped by a "nonanxious presence" in a conflict or other crisis? If so, would you tell about it? Have you ever been the "nonanxious presence" in a conflict or other crisis? If so, reflect on that experience.

9

Further Aids to the Search from Christian Ethics and Theology

> *... There are also truths to be learned from the Christian ethicists and theologians. We all are certain that God's will is a healthy, whole church on mission, and they may offer clues how this may be so ...*

FOR YOUR PERSONAL OR GROUP WORSHIP

Scripture

For he is our peace; in his flesh he has made both groups into one and has broken down the dividing wall of hostility that is between us. He has abolished the law with its commandments and ordinances, that he might create in himself one new humanity in place of the two, thus making peace, and might reconcile both groups to God in one body through the cross, thus putting to death that hostility through it. So he came and preached peace to you who were far and to those who were near; for through him both of us have access in one Spirit to the Father.

So then you are no longer strangers and aliens, but you are citizens with saints and also members of the household of God, built upon the foundation of the apostles and prophets, with Christ Jesus himself as the cornerstone. In him the whole structure is joined together and grows into a holy temple in the Lord; in whom you also are built together spiritually into a dwelling place for God. (Eph 2:19–22)

A Word to Ponder

God is present in each moment when creativity is entertained, when novelty and growth are welcomed, when truth is greeted, when differences are appreciated, when community is celebrated. Part of the mystery of conflict is the mysterious working of the Spirit of God to move a congregation—your congregation—toward something new and better. To be able to find hope in conflict, a leader—in this case, you—needs to be able to see the working of God in the tempests and turmoil of change. (David R. Sawyer)[1]

The most compelling premise of this book [*Negotiating at an Uneven Table*] is that the resolution of human conflicts is *a moral enterprise* that is the responsibility of every human. Norman Cousins, in a legacy to the culture he so valued wrote . . . shortly before he died . . . "Beyond the clamor of clashing ideologies and the preening and jostling of sovereign tribes, a safer and more responsible world is waiting to be created." (Phyllis Kritek)[2]

FOR YOUR THOUGHT AND REFLECTION

I am an untalented but wildly enthusiastic tennis player, one who looks forward to my weekly games with great anticipation. Though I rarely win, I love playing, so much so that I rarely reflect why I like it so much. When I do ponder that question, I become aware that I enjoy being outdoors and like the people I play with. It is fun to be lost in the competition for a while, and exhilarating to make an occasional good shot.

But best of all is how I feel after playing—so relaxed, so drained of tension and hostility. I have flailed away at a little inanimate yellow ball that has no feelings, have swung at it (and usually hit it) many times, have physically expressed any pent-up feelings I may have. And, as the saying goes, I "left it all out on the court."

This experience comes to mind as I continue to pursue an ethic of anger and conflict. As noted earlier, wise counselors have guided us to reject an "anger is sin" perspective. This one says all anger and conflict is evil—avoid, deny, or suppress it. They have also advised against a passive "anger is lord" attitude that says, "Anger and conflict just is. Go with the

---

1. David R. Sawyer, *Hope in Conflict: Discovering Wisdom in Congregational Turmoil*, 160–61.

2. Phyllis Beck Kritek, *Negotiating at an Uneven Table*, 17. Italics added.

flow, let it all hang out, let it rip." A more balanced perspective is needed. But what is it?

In searching for this ethical middle way I considered offering a "tennis theory of anger and conflict." It would provide at least a start. For example, be aware of the angers and conflicts in your life. Get away from them once in a while. Release your tensions in ways that do not harm others. Take care of yourself. Those suggestions are all helpful. But then, my fledgling theory runs out of steam.

It is my hope that each chapter of this book has been a building block in helping you create that broader ethic, strategy, and skillfulness as regards anger and conflict. This chapter may provide another.

I may be inviting you into territory where some of us are not willing to go. That's okay. Feel free to disagree with me. A good part of what Christian ethics is all about is working on disagreements. Indeed, some suggest that the discipline of Christian ethics cannot begin until the legitimacy of differing moral judgments is acknowledged. All I ask you to do is think about it.

I am going to offer a series of statements that I as a Christian ethicist believe. You can decide whether you agree or not and whether any of these statements offer help in our search for better ways of handling our conflicts.

Helpful Distinctions Between Moral and Nonmoral Issues

First, I suggest to you that sometimes we ascribe too much importance to our differences.

In Christian ethics, a distinction is made between two terms, moral and nonmoral.[3] While we all have some sense of what "moral" means, let's consider what "nonmoral" means. It does not mean immoral—the opposite of moral. Rather it means *other than* moral. Sometimes when we describe a person's behavior, we do so in moral terms, "She did the right thing." Sometimes we describe a person's behavior in nonmoral terms, "She is good at that."

When we think about the moral, we think of such things as doing right or wrong, obeying the commands of God, increasing the welfare of other people or of animals or the environment. When we think about the nonmoral, we think of such things as beauty, enjoyment, comfort,

---

3. This distinction exists in philosophical ethics as well. A good discussion of these terms and their importance is provided in William K. Frankena, *Ethics*.

convenience, and custom. As we distinguish between them, these two similar but very different sentences may help—

- Moral: He lived a good life. (That is, he was considerate and righteous in how he lived.)
- Nonmoral: He had a good life. (That is, he experienced desirable things in life—relationships, beauty, and comfort.)

The confusing part is that we often use the same language for moral and for nonmoral decisions. Moral: "You really ought to join us on this petition drive on hunger." Nonmoral: "You really ought to see that movie . . . or buy that car."

Though the two are often hard to distinguish and sometimes mingle, there is an important distinction here. If we then go on and ask, which are the most important in the life of a church, the moral or the nonmoral issues, we would certainly answer the moral ones.

This leads to the thought that often church conflicts (that may develop into major hurtful, long-term battles) are over nonmoral issues. For example in the previous chapter, we spoke of a church that fell apart when the minister rearranged the pews around the communion table. How should the pews be arranged is, in my opinion, a nonmoral issue. Comfort, various concepts of communion, custom, familiarity may all enter in. It certainly seems a resolvable issue. However, it was not so for that church.

With my introductory ethics classes, I offer a series of questions and ask them to identify whether I am speaking of a moral or nonmoral issue. Here are some of my questions: 1. Should the minister wear a robe? 2. Should the benediction be spoken or sung? 3. Should the invitation to Christian discipleship at the close of the service be written or spoken? 4. Should the candidates for membership be baptized (in my denominational tradition) on Palm Sunday? 5. Should a clergy person get married? 6. What should we pay our pastor?

Which descriptive word (moral or nonmoral) would you have given each item on this list? Most of my students see 1–4 as nonmoral, but are not so sure about 5 and 6. On 5, if I am part of a faith tradition where the clergy have made vows of chastity, poverty, and obedience, renouncing those vows is a moral issue. On the other hand, in other faith groups, if it is a desire for greater happiness and companionship, it is probably mostly nonmoral. On 6, if the clergy person struggles with poverty and has difficulty rendering ministry because of lack of financial resources, clergy pay is clearly a moral issue. If the minister has been adequately provided for, it is probably nonmoral.

I find that this distinction gives me some perspective on some of the troubling conflicts that Christians are experiencing, for example, on the topic of worship. The mandate to worship our great God, the centrality of worship for believer and congregation, remembering who is the object of our worship—these are all deeply theological-moral concerns.

However, the *how* of Christian worship may be different. We could continue the list of questions I started earlier: 7. Should worship team or choir lead the worship? 8. Should singers in the worship service wear black robes or black t-shirts? 9. Should the one bringing the message wear robe, suit, or casual clothes? Use manuscript, notes, or nothing written? Speak from a high pulpit, a music stand, or while wandering among the congregation? 10. Shall the music of praise and adoration come from the 19th, 20th, or 21st century? Be accompanied by organ or guitar?

It seems to me that questions around the "how" of worship are nonmoral issues, which we have invested with heavy moral and spiritual freight.

Of course (especially in ethics!), nothing is quite that clear or simple. Though the distinction between moral and nonmoral is important, there are many issues where both sets of considerations enter in. Some of our "how" issues in worship certainly have moral aspects—revitalizing the church, reaching previously unresponsive people, caring for those who have come to love a style of worship. Also, people on both sides of this issue have cherished values to defend and may experience pain if those values are pushed aside. The treatment of each other is also a moral issue.

In other words, I am conceding that some issues have aspects of both the moral and the nonmoral in them. One ethicist suggests that rather than moral-nonmoral, we should instead talk about "moral density."[4] His point is that there is never an issue that is totally devoid of some moral aspect. Of course, neither is there an issue that is ever totally devoid of nonmoral aspects. Sometimes the issue is much more nonmoral, as I am contending the question of worship style is. And sometimes the issue is more morally dense—heavy on the side of deep moral issues.

---

4. James H. Burtness, *Consequences: Morality, Ethics, and the Future*, 37–41.

I am helped to keep potentially conflictual issues in perspective when I see something as mostly a nonmoral issue, even if the person discussing it does not and is highly agitated. This perspective helps me to have that nonanxious presence. In turn, I may be able to hear another person's concerns more clearly and to sort out what is helpful response as we continue responsibly to talk with each other.

However, as helpful as this observation may be, it is of limited help and applies to only a few of the issues that divide us. What further wisdom does Christian ethics-theology offer?

Discovering the Truly Foundational

Second, consider that as Christians, we have a central commitment and loyalty. We hold vital beliefs in common. This opens the door to constructive dialogue about how we should behave.

James H. Burtness, a professor of theology and ethics notes that disagreement is both natural and necessary to the life of the church because of who and what the church is.[5] In the previous chapter, we explored Paul's teaching of the church as the body of Christ as an early way to speak of systems theory. However, these same Bible passages also convey an even more basic truth. We are the body of *Christ.* Christ is the head of the body, the one who directs, relates to, loves, and unites us all. Belief in Christ who unites us is the tie that binds.

While there are movements that bring people of similar background together, that is *not* true of the church. The church often has all the diversity of society at large. Burtness writes, "The only thing that binds the church together is allegiance to Jesus Christ. Male and female, young and old, poor and rich, Republicans and Democrats, married and single—all come together in the church, which binds them to the one body of Christ." This diversity is a test of, and a contribution to the unity of the church. If the diversity were not present, unity in Christ, and in Christ alone, would not be so clear.

This leads him to the conclusion, "Diversity of opinion, even on moral issues, ought to flourish in the church, which locates its center solely in Jesus Christ."[6] While society is seldom certain of its center, the

---

5. James H. Burtness, "When Christians Disagree," *The Lutheran*, August 9, 1989, 12–14.

6. Ibid., 13.

Further Aids to the Search from Christian Ethics and Theology

church is, and thus it can be a place where controversial moral issues can be raised and debated with civility.

To be sure, confusion arises as Christian people of good will begin to translate their faith into appropriate behavior. Part of this faithful response is basic and clear. Almost all Christians agree that faith should lead to loving behavior and that we should work for justice in all matters. (Our survey in chapter six took us that far.) However, specific positions on particular moral or political issues are human judgments. Too often we mistake our human opinions for "truths revealed by God through conscience, whisperings of the Holy Spirit, divinely guided reason, simple reading of isolated biblical texts or automatic dictates of compassion or courage."[7] Whatever our reasons for our beliefs and opinions, they deserve careful examination and discussion.

Burtness calls on fellow believers to claim their basic understanding of the grace of God and unity in Christ as a contribution to ethical dialogue. "The center of our lives is not behavior but belief, not conduct but confession. Therefore, we are free to recognize that our moral judgments are human judgments, not obvious truths."[8] If so, we are free to consider that some of our judgments may need adjusting or even changing. Further, we are free from dismissing those who disagree with us as lacking something essential such as compassion, conscience, character, or common sense.

That is the goal and the task for the church whose unity is in Christ. However, such conversation is not easy and too often does not happen. And so Burtness goes on to offer eight guidelines for such mutually helpful conversations to take place.

1. Assume that:
   - The person with whom you disagree is just as committed both to Christ and to the task of moral reasoning as you are;
   - This person is just as sensitive, compassionate, caring, and just as informed as you;
   - The person with whom you disagree is your moral equal; and
   - Your disagreement is genuine and about matters of moral substance.

7. Ibid.
8. Ibid.

2. "Pay attention to and respond to the content of comments from others."[9] Do not sabotage the conversation by turning it into a set of observations, psychological analysis or accusations about the other person.

3. "Use clear, clean, and neutral language"—as far as it is possible. Recognize the difference between one's opinions and indisputable facts. Do not use slogans or name-calling.

4. "Try to begin with agreement on what the point of contention actually is." It is helpful to discover all the areas in which people actually agree. Where are the points of difference? Define the point(s) of contention as clearly as possible.

5. "Recognize that words seldom have entirely obvious or universal meanings." Discuss how each of the parties uses the important terms in the topic under discussion.

6. Be aware that many of these moral issues are often highly charged emotionally. If one makes upset and passionate accusations, resist the impulse to respond in kind. At the times when there are cries, screams, outbursts in the conversation, do not walk away. Rather let these be occasions for additional patience and generosity.

7. "Give reasons for your opinions that the one with whom you are speaking will find at least interesting." Burtness doubts that appeals to raw authority, conscience, or highly personal experiences are of much help in dialoguing about such disputes. (At this point he differs from the practice in Search for Common Ground, described in chapter 7—those people begin with personal experience in understanding their differences.)

8. Exercise the common human virtue of courtesy. This is the minimum requirement if constructive, clarifying conversation is to take place. He suggests that in this setting, Jesus's Golden Rule might read, "Be as courteous to the one who disagrees with you as you would have that person be to you."[10]

---

9. James H. Burtness, *Consequences,* 157–58.

10. These eight guidelines are found with slight variations from one to the other in "When," 13–14, and *Consequences,* 157–58. The quoted material is directly from those sources.

This author acknowledges the tremendous amount of patience, humility, vulnerability, and patience that is needed in conversations about important moral judgments. However, in this effort there is a double hope: that the church may be able to affirm its unity in the midst of the conflict; and that public discourse about this topic may be transformed by the way the church carries on its discussion.

At the same time, there may need to be help from other sources. For all the good things Burtness had to say, it may have troubled some of us when he spoke of some of our ethical choices as "human judgments." They may feel like more than that to us. These may be cherished values, causes in which we have invested much of ourselves. Yet still we differ with Christian brothers and sisters. What then? Consider this—

A Perspective for Inevitable Conflicts

Third, we are wise to remember that there are valid reasons for our different moral conclusions at times. These reasons call for efforts at understanding, tolerance, and imaginative efforts at continued dialogue. Goodness knows there are invalid reasons. But there are also valid reasons why God's people sometimes differ.

This statement integrates the previous two, but it also takes us further into sensitive territory that needs careful description. Ethicist Edward Stevens can help us here as he names and describes three possible stances on morals-ethics-values. Read and reflect on all three before deciding where you stand.

a) There is *moral relativism*. In this view, many of the answers to any moral dilemma are all equally good. One makes choices by what is most appealing or available or convenient. And there is no requirement to stick with that view if another seems more appealing later on. The payoff for this view is an easy tolerance and acceptance of many different people and views. It comes at a cost of lack of rootedness or moral direction.

b) There is *moral absolutism*. In this view, ". . . [T]here is only one correct morality, I possess it, and everyone else is wrong."[11] Absolutism has many payoffs as well—certitude, moral superiority, political effectiveness, and a sense of moral purity.

---

11. Edward Stevens, *Developing Moral Imagination: Case Studies in Practical Morality*, vii.

However, these benefits also come at a high price. Stevens writes, "Absolutists must deliberately blind themselves to important moral values that scream out for attention and response." And further, "Absolutists maintain the lie by demonizing the opposition."[12] He points out that there are absolutists on both sides of every moral dilemma, including those issues that are tearing the church apart.

As Stevens looks for an alternative to either of these, he notes the fact of (c) *moral pluralism*. There are indeed many different and alternative moral views competing for one's assent. This does not mean that they all are equally good or acceptable. Out of this fact, Stevens suggests a stance of *moral pluralism* as the needed alternative.

At this point we need to be careful with the term "moral pluralism" and be sure we are all talking about the same thing. Some see it is almost the same as the definition of moral relativism given above. In this connection, we might recall the caution offered by Martin Marty, "One of the real problems in modern life is that people who are good at being civil often lack strong convictions, and people who have strong convictions often lack civility."[13] Dennis Hollinger cautions that tolerance at the cost of faithful conviction and commitment is perilous to a faithful Christian ethic. Then he goes on to examine Christian strategy within the fact of an increasingly secular and pluralistic culture.[14] The danger of confusing moral relativity and moral pluralism is real, and the broad cultural context in which pluralism is a fact of life is also real.

However, Stevens neither falls into that trap, nor is his primary concern that wider cultural context. Rather he seeks a helpful stance for persons within the faith community to carry on helpful ethical conversation with each other. He contends that we Christian believers have a moral

---

12. Ibid., 137.

13. Dennis Hollinger, *Choosing the Good*, 116. He is quoting Marty, *By Way of Response*, 81.

14. Ibid. In chapter 11, 238–55, Hollinger speaks helpfully of Christian ethical strategies in a pluralistic culture. He points to the options of privatization of religion, a theocratic-Constantinian approach, a civil religion response, or faithful Christian witness and influence within pluralism. He favors the latter, noting that Christians will need to be "bilingual" at times, speaking the language of Zion to fellow believers, and a broader language to the culture at large.

Further Aids to the Search from Christian Ethics and Theology   141

pluralism among ourselves, and this deserves to be acknowledged, addressed, and encouraged.

Stevens points out that the position of pluralism does not agree with relativism. The pluralist believes deeply and strongly that some things are right and some are wrong and that one should vigorously debate, defend, and practice what one believes. The pluralist believes there are moral truths and these can be defended as true.

At the same time, the pluralist also rejects the opposite extreme of absolutism. The pluralist tries to make valid ethical judgments without being judgmental. The pluralist believes that moral beliefs are true, but at the same time they are limited, partial, and incomplete. And so the pluralist defends one's own views while attempting to deepen and complement them in dialogue with other moral views. We do have finite minds, cultural filters, and our language is limited. So the search for the deeper, more comprehensive truth is a valid, faithful, and vital search.[15]

Stevens wholeheartedly agrees with Laurence Hinman, whom he quotes:

> Absolutism fails to offer a convincing account of how opposing people could be both well informed and good intentioned. It says there is only one answer, and those who do not see it are either ignorant or ill willed. Relativism fails to offer a convincing account of how people can agree. It says no one is wrong.
>
> There is a third possible response, *moral pluralism*. Moral pluralists maintain that there are moral truths, but they do not form a body of coherent and consistent truths in the way that one finds in science or mathematics. Moral truths are real, but partial.[16]

What then are the valid reasons we sometimes differ from each other? They are many, and we have spoken of most of them. They include our varied cultural backgrounds and family histories, church backgrounds, personality types, interests, and sympathies.

Charles Kimball expresses this awareness of himself when he writes,

> The fact that I was born in 1950 and raised in Tulsa, Oklahoma, in the midst of the post—World War II baby boom—as opposed

---

15. These paragraphs are a summary of Stevens's thoughts, vi–x and 134–42.

16. Ibid., v. He is quoting Laurence Hinman, *Contemporary Moral Issues: Diversity and Consensus*, 3.

to Bombay or Cairo or Tokyo or Boston, as were my Jewish cousins—makes a substantial difference in my religious orientation to the world. My background and worldview shape the way I frame religious questions. This is not bad or wrong. It does mean that my experiences and understanding of God—however powerful and life changing these have been—do not exhaust all the possibilities.[17]

We might add that the ethical conclusions that Kimball makes out of this context do not exhaust the possibilities either.

The surprise is not that we have many differences in the church; rather the wonder is that we come so close to mutuality and consensus once in a while. (And, as I just affirmed, we gather around a common Core.) The reasons for our differences are valid, and the concept of moral pluralism helps us see that. That doesn't mean we renounce or ignore any deep moral conviction. It does mean we keep our differences in manageable perspective and keep working on them.

A Christian Strategy When All Else Fails

And fourth, it is essential to claim a central gift of our faith, namely forgiveness and reconciliation. This is also one of the most basic responsibilities to each other we are given as followers of Christ. Our God of generous grace is a God of forgiveness and reconciliation, and this truth has relevance to our divisions and conflicts.

In the New Testament, we are reminded again and again of God's lavish favor upon us, in creation, in forgiveness, in redemption, in reconciliation. But not only that, we are called upon to express this reconciling grace to each other. In one of Jesus's parables, the master who had forgiven a servant of a huge debt asks him, "I forgave all that debt because you pleaded with me. Should you not have had mercy on your fellow slave as I had mercy on you?" (Matt. 18:32b–33).

Similarly in Ephesians we who have been reconciled to each other and to God are summoned—"Put away from you all bitterness and wrath and anger and wrangling and slander, together with all malice, and be kind to one another, tenderhearted, forgiving one another as God in Christ has forgiven you. Therefore be imitators of God, as beloved children, and live in love, as Christ loved us and gave himself up for us, a fragrant offering and sacrifice to God" (Eph 4:31—5:2).

---

17. Charles Kimball, *When Religion Becomes Evil*, 67.

Further Aids to the Search from Christian Ethics and Theology   143

Certainly we are to act in this way when we have *been wronged*. But what about the times when we have honest differences? Can you forgive me for *being wrong*? I may not be repentant. In fact, I may still be convinced of my position, with which you, in your attempt to be faithful totally disagree. Even then, can you love me, pray for me, keep fellowship with me, and keep talking with me? God did not wait for me to be deserving to reach out to me in reconciling love. Can you do the same for me?

That may be our best hope of all in all of our struggles with each other. But we will speak more of such matters in the next chapter.

QUESTIONS AND ACTIVITIES FOR GROUP REFLECTION

1. Do you agree with my analysis of moral and nonmoral issues? What about the idea that some issues are more "morally dense" than others? In what ways can this concept be helpful in the conflicts you face? Can you think of conflicts you have experienced that are over nonmoral subjects? If so, what are they?

2. What is your response to James Burtness's understanding of the church as a widely diverse people who know their Center, and thus have the power to disagree agreeably? Have you experienced the church that way? If yes, tell the others about it. If no, are you drawn toward that vision?

3. Which of James Burtness's guidelines for constructive dialogue are you already practicing? Which of those you do not practice seem possible to you? Which seem idealistic and beyond any discussion or conflict you have experienced?

4. State the concepts of moral relativity, moral absolutism, and moral pluralism in your own language. Think about the five most frequently discussed moral dilemmas in your experience. On which of these issues are you morally absolute? On which morally relative? On which morally pluralist? If you have some in each these categories, can you explain why?

5. What do you think of the idea of forgiving someone who differs from you on some of these issues? Have you ever experienced that—either giving or receiving the forgiveness? If so, would you tell the group about it?

10

What if—in Spite of All Our Efforts— We Are Still at Odds?

. . . But, you ask, what if after doing all this, we still have deep, intractable differences? Then we are called back to our basic beliefs— that God loves us, that Christ died and rose for us, and that those who believe are family of faith. Our conflict is with family of faith members, and this is our most basic reality. It is better to be respectful, considerate family members even with significant differences, than to be quarreling ones. Through the love that streams from the cross, there is always another way.

So, I urge you, stand by your basic convictions, but have a clear understanding of what is primary and what is secondary in our community of believers. In God's house, there are many abiding places, and we have room for many differences . . .

FOR YOUR PERSONAL OR GROUP WORSHIP

Scripture

He said to them, "Wherever you enter a house, stay there until you leave the place. If any place will not welcome you and they refuse to hear you, as you leave, shake off the dust that is on your feet as a testimony against them." (Mark 6:10–11)

Jerusalem, Jerusalem, the city that kills the prophets and stones those who are sent to it! How often have I desired to gather your children together as a hen gathers her brood under her wings, and you were not willing! (Matt 23:37)

What has become of the good will you felt? For I testify that had it been possible, you would have torn out your eyes and given them to me. Have I now become your enemy by telling you the truth? . . . My little children, for whom I am again in the pain of childbirth until Christ is formed in you, I wish I were present with you now and could change my tone, for I am perplexed about you. (Gal 4:15–16, 19–20)

A Word to Ponder

The Protestant theologian Shirley C. Guthrie says each of us is a theologian whether we want to be or not, and he says the best theologians are modest about what they think they know about God.

Modesty is not, unfortunately, a stance our culture encourages. In a time of self-assertiveness, of a sexually explicit entertainment industry, of political aggressiveness that employs the lie as a primary tool of communication, of pro sports that pay individual show-offs the most money—in a time of all this and more, modesty about what we believe is viewed as weakness, as timidity, as foolishness.

Instead, our in-your-face world encourages the *Deus le volt!* ["God wills it"—the battle cry of the Crusades] that drove the Crusaders to commit murder for God.

Our failure to find a new way to live after all these centuries is ruinous. (Bill Tammeus)[1]

FOR YOUR THOUGHT AND REFLECTION

Like other people of good will, Christians of different persuasions may discover that all of our efforts toward mutual understanding and agreement do not succeed. We have tried, but we can neither let go of our convictions nor convince the others to let go of theirs. What then?

Lynne McClure, who has written helpfully about anger and conflict in the workplace offers us a place to start with her seventh skill—letting go. (Her first six skills are: 1. Decide whether both you and the other want to work things out; 2. Acknowledge feelings, before getting to facts, issues, and opinions; 3. Discover something you and the other have in common; 4. Identify the genuine issues, not the presenting or apparent ones and not the details; 5. Depersonalize the issue and see it in perspec-

---

1. Bill Tammeus, "Theologically Speaking, Modesty Would Help Us All," B7.

tive from a variety of angles; and 6. Be purposive and direct, going to the appropriate person with your goals and purposes.)[2]

Those first six skills used ably with good will can certainly reduce differences, decrease friction, and often resolve conflict. We have born witness and advocated for such efforts in the preceding chapters. However, when even these fail, McClure suggests yet one other skill—letting go. Very basically this means recognizing what is out of your hands and up to the other party. Of course, there are many painful feelings that are part of letting go:

- Helplessness, for there is nothing else one can do;
- Sadness that comes with lost opportunities;
- Fear that comes with the awareness of how little control we have in our lives;
- Guilt, sensing the other's refusal might be connected to something I did; and
- Anger out of frustrated goals and desires.[3]

These are all hurtful emotions, to be sure. However, when an impossible impasse has been experienced, the long-term pain is less and the health is greater if one faces this fact deeply and honestly, and then lets go.

How does one learn to let go? Here is McClure's guidance:

- Take steps to do what you can—such as using the anger management skills.
- Admit, to yourself, that you feel hurt, disappointed, sad—or whatever you feel when things don't go your way.
- Let yourself feel the pain, without doing anything about it. This helps you let go of the urge—or the need—to control it.
- Give others the space to make their own choices. This helps you let go of the urge to control *them*.

---

2. McClure, *Anger and Conflict in the Workplace: Spot the Signs, Avoid the Trauma*, 28–71.

3. Ibid., 73–74.

- Get on with what you have, and learn to do with what you don't have. Letting go will make it easier to manage your own and others' anger.[4]

As helpful as McClure's guidance is, we need to translate it from the work place to local congregations and to denominations. What does "letting go" mean in the church? Does it mean claming up and withdrawing from conversation, or perhaps physically vacating oneself from a church? Does it mean excommunicating or expelling those with whom one disagrees?

Clearly, any of those behaviors would be clear signs of *not having let go* of the conflict yet. Indeed, McClure's assumption from the workplace is that all of the contestants in the conflict will still be employed at the same place, or at least within the same firm and, very likely, need to deal with each other time and again in the future.

We might find ourselves confused about this letting go because of one of Jesus's words to his disciples. Jesus did indeed tell the disciples he sent out with his message to the surrounding villages, that if the village does not welcome them to shake the dust off their feet as they leave as a witness (Mark 6:10–11). Persons have spoken of that act as the "sacrament of failure," or the "ordinance of closure."

There may be such times when Christian persons must reluctantly withdraw from each other. Many of us have experienced such heartbreaking times as well as the pain and sadness that went with it. But this verse should be seen in context and not too easily claimed for withdrawal from those with whom one has differences. When Jesus spoke those words, he was sending disciples out on brief, urgent journeys proclaiming God's dawning kingdom. In that setting, there was little time to devote to unresponsive communities.

Balanced over against that saying is Jesus's lamenting because of Jerusalem's unresponsiveness (Matt 23:37) as well as Paul's longing for reconciliation with the Galatians (Gal 4:15–20), both communities from which they experienced much resistance and estrangement.

Letting go within the family of God in times of deep conflict needs clear understanding and appropriate actions. So what are we to do when we still differ with each other? There are at least five possibilities. You can decide how many of these possibilities are fitting for you.

---

4. Ibid., 78–79.

Make Some Important Distinctions

For one thing, we can separate where we differ from where we do not. Some years ago, I was active as a part of a clergy group working for school desegregation in the community where I lived. There were many public meetings, often with the school board, and these usually did not go the way we hoped.

Most of us would be rather discouraged at such times. However, one of our number, Gene Boutilier, would respond differently, often with understanding of why board decisions were made. He would then come up with ideas for improving their plan so that it would include the items we thought important. And, he didn't lose his enthusiam for what we were doing.

I so appreciated the perspective and strategies that Gene brought to our effort, that one day I asked him to explain how he did it. He responded by telling a story. Before coming to our community, he had been a lobbyist for Cesar Chavez's National Farm Workers Association. From time to time, Gene would appear before a congressional sub-committee along with his opponent, the lobbyist for owners and employers. Both persons would argue forcefully for their group's point of view as well as criticize and attack positions held by the other side. This would become quite heated.

At the end of the day, as he and his opponent walked out together, they might discover they lived in the same part of the city and share a taxi going home! "There's a difference between structural conflict and personal conflict," Gene told me. "We will do our best work if we keep the two separate." His wisdom was sound; it made for more inner serenity as well as better relations with those on the other side of the issue.

Incidentally, in that same campaign, our clergy committee included a Wisconsin Synod Lutheran pastor named Tom. When we planned a citywide gathering of clergy to rally support for our desegregation efforts, Tom apologetically asked if we would mind not praying at that meeting. Clergy of his denomination would feel free to attend a meeting dealing addressing a community concern with other clergy. However, they were not open to worshipping with them!

We gave our consent—again the conflict was structural, not personal. Gene equipped us with a sound perspective: distinguish between structural and personal conflict; separate where we differ from where we do not.

Discern What Is Primary and What Is Secondary

Further, we can discover what we hold in common as well as where we differ. I once had some very strong differences with a man who was engaged to one of my daughters. (Of course, no one is good enough for my daughters, but this was something more and different). He married my daughter anyway.

In time a baby was born to this couple, a little girl. Both her father and I love that child with unconditional, unabashed love. We think she's great, will do anything to aid her growth and discovery, and are absolutely committed to her best. As persons of integrity, we will not compete but rather support and supplement each other in offering what is good for that child (who is now a young woman).

Over the years our relationship with each other has grown even though we probably still disagree on the subjects we debated and argued back then. Only now, they don't seem so important. In fact, they are a far second to our joy in our daughter-granddaughter, this person who binds us together in mutual concern.

And when you and I differ on a topic, we need to do a similar thing. In our opening section of this chapter, McClure spoke of finding something in common with the other. For Christians, this is essential for we have so much in common. We share belief/trust in God as we have known God through Christ and experienced God in the presence of the Holy Spirit.

In a conflict between you and me, I am not arguing with a stranger, but a family member—a sister or brother. Our loyalty to our creating and redeeming God, and God's love for all God's children (including you, my competitor) puts our conflict in perspective. Our differences need to be set in proper perspective of the magnificent realities we hold in common.

Part of what we hold in common is church, which the New Testament images as Christ's body and Christ's family. We share love for the church and responsibility to act in its best welfare. We need a clear distinction between what is primary and what is secondary in our conflicted relationship.

Perhaps I can further illustrate this distinction with reference to an ethical dilemma of another generation. Years ago, ministerial candidates were sometimes asked, "Do you believe in dancing?" I have heard of different answers given by two different ministers that both evaded and illuminated that question. In response to the query, "Do you believe in dancing?" one minister responded, "I never found it necessary for salvation." The other answered, "Yes, I've seen them do it!"

Both answers make this distinction; they strongly imply that a question starting with "Do you believe in" is too big a question to end with "dancing." That question should be saved for the big, the basic, foundational questions. Do you believe in—God? Do you believe in Jesus Christ as Lord and Savior? Do you believe in the church as Christ's body and Christ's family? These questions are primary.

The question about dancing—or other debatable behaviors—is secondary and should be stated such. A much better question would be—do you believe that it is morally fitting for a Christian to dance? Then it is not a question of Christian basics and is open to the discussion that important, but secondary topics deserve.

Make Mission Central

And again, it is important to affirm that the mission is more compelling than the conflict.

When I was a teenager, I worked on farms during the summers. In August of my junior year, two brothers, Nick and Jake Schmidt who had adjoining farms hired me to help in the harvest of small grains.

One day when we were harvesting oats on Jake's farm, we stopped at noon and went into Jake's house to eat. Over dessert and coffee, Nick and Jake started talking-debating politics. (Nick was a committed "New Deal" Democrat; Jake an equally committed Republican). I was chuckling as they began, for they knew their positions, were quick on the comeback, and didn't lack for humorous asides.

Family members grew tense, however. I later learned that everyone tried to keep these two off this topic. Too quickly, they left the humor and play behind, and the argument grew more and more heated. At the height of a shouting match, Nick couldn't take it any more. He stood up, took off his cap and slung it to the floor with all the might of his frustration. He then picked it up, went out—and started his combine to finish harvesting his brother's oats.

If we had concentrated more on the harvest, this argument need not have been re-experienced. Since it did arise, Nick had the good sense to withdraw from the fight and turn to the urgent task at hand—harvest the grain before it spoiled or a storm destroyed it.

I often think of Nick and Jake in view of the present conflicts in the church. In chapter six, I reported on responses to a small survey I undertook as a beginning step in a search for our most basic mandate-mission in the present century. Though much more needs to be done, the responses moved us in the direction of clarity about that mission. If we concentrate on the mission with our effort and resources, I am convinced we will argue less. And, if our arguments divert us, awareness of the harvest and other mission tasks that await us may draw us back from the conflict and into the mission.

When Necessary, Practice Civil and Fair Conflict.

Further, we can follow this principle: When in conflict, do it in a respectful + fitting = Christian manner. In his book, *Uncommon Decency: Christian Civility in an Uncivil World*, Richard Mouw notes how the various theories of war—holy war or crusade, just war, no war—become a part of how we deal with each other on issues where we differ.

He points out that that when we are deeply convicted on some subject, we all have something of the crusader (the holy war mentality) in us. When we give that crusader spirit free rein, we may ignore such things as accuracy, consideration for the opponent, or civility. That may be left behind in search of helping one's cause triumph. And so when entering a conflict, Mouw offers a rule of thumb, "*For starters, concentrate on your own sinfulness and on the other person's humanness.* We become more civil by gaining a more honest picture of ourselves and others."[5]

Mouw goes on to suggest that when we indeed need to do conflict on some subject, that some of the insights of "just war" theory might guide us. Here are the questions he helpfully suggests:

"*Is my cause a just one?*" Before launching this debate, I might well consider and ponder Ps. 139:23, "Search me, O God and know my heart; test me and know my thoughts."

"*Am I sustained in my commitments by the wisdom of competent authorities?*" Have I sought the counsel of the wider Christian body?

"*Are my motives proper?*" It is important to pay careful attention not only to what we are trying to accomplish but also our reasons for wanting to do so.

---

5. Richard Mouw, *Uncommon Decency: Christian Civility in an Uncivil World*, 55. Italics are his.

"Is my move beyond civility a choice of last resort?" There needs to be thoroughness in choosing strategies. Is there any possible win-win strategy? Have we exhausted all other possibilities for resolution?

"Is success likely?" And what is success? Perhaps it is not so much to overcome the opposition as to maintain one's moral and spiritual integrity.

"Are the means I am employing proportionate to the good goals I want to promote?" We are accountable to God for our actions. While we cannot predict all the outcomes of our decisions, we need to think carefully about them. Even if I win this battle, will it do more harm than good?[6]

Then Mouw goes on to remind us that St. Augustine, who wrote much on just war, also urged kindness in war. In combat, this would include treating prisoners humanely, respecting the rights of civilian populations and more. In our church conflicts, there also needs to be kindness, gentleness, respect for the other person as person, and grace.[7]

William Tillman, Jr., takes this question of how people of differing viewpoints should treat each other a step further. In an essay exploring biblical models for the church's response to homosexuality in the 21st century, he suggests the image of Christ as the transformer of culture. This image is taken from H. Richard Niebuhr's *Christ and Culture,* and Tillman suggests it is a helpful perspective for this dialogue.

In this connection he notes, "To live life from the perspective of Christ as the transformer of culture will mean addressing some matters that perhaps one would rather leave unaddressed."[8] His essay guides congregations in dialoguing with each other with a "biblically-centered" approach, that is, with the goal of shedding more light than heat. Important for our conversation at this point are his concluding words, "You call yourself a Christian; how do you think a Christian should deal with such issues as homosexuality? As you deal with these matters, are you becoming a better Christian for having dealt with them? Is your congregation becoming more Christ-like in doing so?"[9]

---

6. Ibid., 126–31. The questions in italics are direct quotes, which he discusses more thoroughly.

7. Ibid., 131–32.

8. William Tillman, Jr., "The Church's Response to Homosexuality: Biblical Models for the 21st Century," 255.

9. Ibid., 256.

It is wise to examine self and resolve to treat those with whom one disagrees with courtesy and respect. After all, at most, our "war" with each other is a just war. But Tillman takes us a step further—look on this whole controversy, whatever it is, as an opportunity to grow spiritually, to become more Christ-like as individuals and congregations.

Keep Talking and Wait for More Light

After we have done all the things suggested in this chapter and still are at odds, what are we to do then? We keep talking with each other. This truth came home to me when I read an essay by ethicist Nancy J. Duff in a collection written by Princeton Seminary faculty on various perspectives on homosexuality.

Duff's essay is entitled, "How to Discuss Moral Issues Surrounding Homosexuality When You Know You Are Right." She says she is among those who encounter no moral dilemmas in the issues on this topic as she has thought this through, made her decisions and has taken her stand firmly. Duff acknowledges that others who totally disagree with her have done the same thing, have equally strong feelings, and also have no moral dilemmas on this topic. With this impasse, her strong temptation to let it be that way and ignore the opposition is strong.

However, an unlikely source caused her to question this fairly rigid stance. The unlikely source was a nineteenth-century secular philosopher, John Stuart Mill. In his essay "On Liberty," Mill offers three reasons to listen to opposing points of view even when convinced of the correctness of one's own position.

First, Mill suggests "*because we are fallible, if we silence an opposing opinion we may be silencing the truth.*" Given our fallibility, one chance of rectifying our mistakes and compensating for our errors is through discussion and experience. There is a significant distinction between the belief that an opinion is true because it has withstood opposition or that an opinion is true because it has stifled all opposing viewpoints.

Second, Mill suggests that even if the opposing viewpoint is in error, "*it may contain a portion of truth.*" Truth is often discovered by the collision of adverse opinions. If we cut off from each other we both lose the opportunity to correct and improve our own position as well as the opportunity to convince the opponent to correct and improve that opinion.

And third, even if our position is not only true but wholly true, *"it risks becoming no more than prejudice or recitation if it refuses to be in conversation with other opinions."* The one whose conclusions can be trusted is the one who has listened carefully to a wide variety of opposing viewpoints.[10]

Duff reminds us that this guidance coincides with the gospel and its counsel to disagree in love. We need to let go our fear that the other side would win the day and learn to be able to recognize the other side as truly Christian.

I experienced this sort of respectful listening and responding as I read Stanley Grenz's *Welcoming but Not Affirming: An Evangelical Response to Homosexuality* and responses to it. At the outset of this book, Grenz states his thesis that the mandate from our Lord calls the church to welcome all people, including homosexual persons into its fellowship. But, Grenz also believes that the same mandate prohibits the church from condoning same-sex sexual behavior or sexual union.[11] He finds this to be not only the church's historic position but the biblical one, a position to be held unless compelling evidence proves otherwise.

As Grenz proceeds with his analysis, again and again he investigates the writings that offer recent scholarship both on sexuality and on analysis of relevant biblical passages. From my knowledge of such writings, he summarizes accurately, quotes in context and treats each argument fairly. Then he asks if these findings provide reason to abandon the historical church position and gospel mandates as he understands them. And he answers no.

An evangelical scholar, he carries on a respectful listening and analysis with challenges to his position, but his conclusion is that these do not challenge it enough to require changing his position. Grenz did that of which Mills spoke, and, as a result, offers a reasoned, defensible and discussable statement of his position on this difficult and complex topic.

I was equally interested as I looked at the testimonials on the back cover of the book. One of the scholars with a different point of view

---

10. Nancy J. Duff, "How to Discuss Moral Issues Surrounding Homosexuality When You Know You are Right," 144–47. The quotes are from this essay, the italics hers. She in turn is citing and summarizing John Stuart Mill, *On Liberty*.

11. Stanley Grenz, *Welcoming But Not Affirming: An Evangelical Response to Homosexuality*, 1–2.

is James Nelson, and Grenz examined Nelson's views at more than one place within the book. Among the testimonials was one by this same James Nelson who wrote, "I strongly disagree with Stanley Grenz's major conclusions at virtually every point. Nevertheless, I can highly commend this book to those who, like me, are both welcoming *and* affirming. Why? Simply because it is the clearest, fairest presentation of the nonaffirming position yet written, and it is enormously important that all of us stay in constructive, informed dialogue."[12] Nelson also did that of which Mills spoke, both to his own benefit and those for whom he writes.

And so, when still in disagreement we keep talking, but with hope. We have not finished this story. Our God has not written the last chapter on the church, God's creation, and the object of God's joy and love. We are to be as loving, as open, as clear, as true to God's leading as we understand it as we can be, confident that more light and truth will be revealed.

QUESTIONS AND ACTIVITIES FOR GROUP REFLECTION

1. Do you admire someone—perhaps personally known to you, perhaps a public figure—with whom you frequently disagree? If so, how do you hold the admiration and disagreement together?

2. Do you have friendships that also include frequent disagreements? If so, what impact does friendship have on disagreements? What impact do disagreements have on the friendship?

3. In this chapter, I have suggested five ways to deal with other Christian folks with whom you disagree. Which of these seemed most helpful to you? Least helpful? Why? Which of these seemed most possible to you?

4. What stories do you have to tell about people who differed but who continued to care about each other?

5. What further suggestions do you have to respond to the question of this chapter: What if—in spite of all our efforts—we are still at odds?

---

12. Ibid., back cover.

11

A Healing Balm to the Nations: Activating Our Moral and Spiritual Imagination

. . . In closing, I remind you of that prayer Jesus offered for those of us who would come to believe through the word of his disciples. Jesus prayed "that they may all be one. As you, Father, are in me and I am in you, may they also be one in us so that the world may believe that you have sent me" (John 17:21).

A united, loving church will be a witness to the world that God sent Jesus. This healed and gracious church will have both the moral authority and the spiritual energy to be a caring presence in the troubled and conflicted spots in our world and society. What a joy it will be to be part of that healing . . .

FOR YOUR PERSONAL OR GROUP WORSHIP

Scripture

I ask not only on behalf of these, but also on behalf of those who will believe in me through their word, that they may all be one. As you, Father, are in me and I am in you, may they also be in us, so that the world may believe that you have sent me. The glory that you have given me I have given them, so that they may be one, as we are one, I in them and you in me, so that they may become completely one, so that the world may know that you have sent me and have loved them even as you have loved me. (John 17:20–23)

A Word to Ponder

Bishop Tutu speaks of the reconciling spirit when change of government finally came to South Africa, which had been so tragically divided with much bloodshed:

> What is it that constrained so many to choose to forgive rather than to demand retribution, to be so magnanimous and ready to forgive rather than wreak revenge?
>
> *Ubuntu* is very difficult to render into a Western language. It speaks of the very essence of being human. When we want to give high praise to someone we say, *"Yu U nobuntu"*; "Hey, so-and-so has *ubuntu.*" Then you are generous, you are hospitable, you are friendly and caring and compassionate. You share what you have. It is to say, "My humanity is caught up, is inextricably bound up, in yours." We belong to a bundle of life. We say, "A person is a person through other persons." It is not, "I think therefore I am." It says rather: "I am human because I belong. I participate, I share." A person with *ubuntu* is open and available to others, affirming of others, does not feel threatened that others are able and good, for he or she has a proper self-assurance that comes from knowing that he or she belongs in a greater whole and is diminished when others are humiliated or diminished, when others are tortured or oppressed, or treated as if they were less than who they are.
>
> Harmony, friendliness, community are great goods. Social harmony is for us the *summum bonum*—the greatest good. Anything that subverts, that undermines this sought-after good is to be avoided like the plague. Anger, resentment, lust for revenge, even success through aggressive competitiveness are corrosive of this good. To forgive is not just to be altruistic. It is the best form of self-interest. What dehumanizes you inexorably dehumanizes me. It gives people resilience, enabling them to survive and emerge still human despite all efforts to dehumanize them. (Bishop Desmond Tutu)[1]

FOR YOUR THOUGHT AND REFLECTION

One of the most profoundly moving books I have ever read is *No Future Without Forgiveness* by Bishop Desmond Tutu of South Africa. This book contains his reflecting on the tempestuous, yet healing years when the Republic of South Africa left behind its apartheid stance and formed a new government with a new constitution.

---

1. Desmond Tutu, *No Future Without Forgiveness*, 31–32.

He begins by recalling April 27, 1994, the first time in his sixty-two years he could vote. Though there had been fears that some would disrupt the elections, it proved not to be so. Rather, it was a day of celebration. He recalls the amazing and inspiring spectacle of people of all the races standing together in the same line, waiting to vote. The long waits proved to be blessing, not disaster. As they waited, people started talking, sharing newspapers, getting sandwiches for each other. And as he describes it, "Scales began to fall from their eyes." Those long waits "produced a new and peculiarly South African status symbol. Afterward people boasted 'I stood for two hours to vote.' 'I waited for four hours.'"

In those long waits, he said, "South Africans found fellow South Africans—they realized what we had been at such pains to tell them, that they shared a common humanity, that race, ethnicity, skin color were really irrelevancies. They discover not a Colored, a black, an Indian, a white. No, they found fellow human beings."[2]

Such was the rebirth of this nation. However, after the exhilaration of the election, there were harsh realities to be faced. This nation had endured much repression, violence, blood shed in the past. There were known and unknown killings, harassments, damaging and seizing of property. How should this violence—imposed by members of various races on each other—be addressed in this emerging nation?

Two possibilities were proposed. One suggestion was that there be a general amnesty for everything that happened before the new elections. Let bygones be bygones, no matter how harsh, cruel, or unjust those bygones may be. The other possibility was to initiate a new version of the Nuremberg trials, in which war criminals were tried after World War II.

Wisely, the leaders rejected both of these proposals. There was too much suffering and injustice to pretend it never happened or to try to forget it without reexamining these painful experiences. General amnesty was out of the question.

But so was a new round of Nuremberg trials. Those were the trials in international courts of law of leaders of a defeated country. The numbers of those tried at that time were relatively few compared to widespread incidents that South Africa needed to consider.

Instead, they created the Truth and Reconciliation Commission, a plan used by other countries before them, but uniquely adapted to their need. The plan was this—persons guilty of these crimes would

---

2. Ibid., 6–7.

be granted amnesty if they came forward to the commission, and, in the presence of the families of their victims, made a full and truthful disclosure. The victims' families were free to speak for or against amnesty, but this would not determine whether it was granted. Those who confessed were not required to express remorse, but only to make a full and truthful disclosure (an aspect that Tutu questioned at the beginning, but later saw its wisdom). Further these would be public hearings, both for South African citizens and for representatives of the media. (Indeed, there was much news coverage and more than one film documentary of these proceedings.)

Why would those who engaged in such activities make disclosure? The lure was the possibility of freedom in exchange for truth telling, and this was offered both to those already in jail and those who otherwise might face future prosecution.

In addition to full disclosure, there were other conditions laid down. The act under investigation must have happened between 1960, the year of the Sharpeville massacre, and 1994 when President Mandela was inaugurated. The act must have been politically motivated. And, the rubric of proportionality had to apply—that is that the means used in the act had to be proportional to the objective.[3]

At a time when he was anticipating retirement, Bishop Tutu was appointed by President Mandela to be chair of this commission. He felt that this was a duty he could not refuse his president and accepted the appointment. The commission he headed then engaged in eighteen arduous months of hearings.

Space does not allow retelling the many stories members of the commission heard. Tutu acknowledges that more than he expected victims and their family members attested to relief and healing by being able to tell their stories. They so needed to have their sorrow and anger acknowledged and addressed. For many, this was necessary before they could move on with new life in the new republic.

He vividly recalls and tells of the shock, pain, and revulsion he and so many felt when victims spoke of the inhumanity with which they were treated. But he was even more deeply touched by the "resilience of the human spirit" that he saw in persons whose stories were finally told.

He wrote, "We have been moved to tears. We have laughed. We have been silent and we have stared the beast of our dark past in the eye.

3. Ibid., 49–50.

We have survived the ordeal and we are realizing that we can indeed transcend the conflicts of the past, we can hold hands as we realize our common humanity. . . . Forgiveness will follow confession and healing will happen, and so contribute to national unity and reconciliation."[4]

During the time the commission was holding hearings, in 1997, Tutu learned he had prostate cancer. However, he recalled, his cancer helped him to be a little more "laid back" because he realized "there was literally not enough time to be nasty."[5]

He points out that the commission was not perfect and certainly was not without mistakes. Response and participation was not nearly as widespread as they hoped. In spite of their recommendations, little progress was made on some of the harshest results of apartheid, namely the wide difference in economic circumstance of people after it ended. Some still enjoyed the benefits of those years of privilege, and some still suffered from its deprivations.

And yet, as a nation, they acknowledged their painful and bloody past. They heard confession and summoned a mighty spirit of reconciliation. Their nation remembered, acknowledged, healed and moved toward unity.

I urge you to read this story for yourself, for there are so many moving accounts, so much more he told that speak to our search in this book. Do not quit reading too soon, for when you come to the last chapter, you will find one more significant discovery.

It is this—that after Tutu and the Truth and Reconciliation Commission had finished its important work, this leader was invited to many troubled places in the world to speak of their work and to offer hope and guidance. For example, he journeyed to Ireland where he told audiences in Belfast and Dublin that the South African experience showed that "almost no situation could be said to be devoid of hope." He recalls "They heard this message as if in a sense it had been uttered by an oracle."[6] Not only there, but in several other countries, where he spoke, he sensed that this process—so honestly and painfully engaged lent credibility to what he had to say. In this regard, his journeys took him to Rwanda, Ireland, Israel, and Palestine.

---

4. Ibid., 119–20.
5. Ibid., 287.
6. Ibid., 261, 262.

And so this gifted Christian leader continues to apply his bold spirituality of forgiveness and reconciliation wherever the need arises, years after he thought he would start his retirement! Undertaking the essential task of reconciliation in his country has given Bishop Tutu (and other South African leaders) both the moral authority and the spiritual energy to make a contribution in new situations that so desperately need a different way!

I take inspiration and discovery from this story. It is a needed one for us church folks today. Too often the churches these days do not have the impact in troubled and divisive areas of our world that we might wish.

The reason for this lack of influence is at least twofold. For one, we lack moral authority, and this is due, at least in part, to our troubled relationships with each other. We are called to be agents of reconciliation, but too often, we are tragically and publicly divided among ourselves.

For the other, we lack the spiritual energy because we have depleted our inner selves arguing over secondary matters. A renewal and revival of God's mighty spirit among us is needed. I am convinced that at least one source of this renewal will be when we embrace each other, forgive each other, and claim what unity we can with integrity. Then we can stand together, revitalized by God's spirit to be, as a hymn so beautifully puts it, "... a healing balm to the nations."

Bishop Tutu's story led me to think more deeply about a foundational scripture passage—the seventeenth chapter of John. In chapters 13–17 of his gospel, John describes Jesus's last teaching of the disciples. It is preparation for a new and different day—the time after his death and resurrection. These chapters begin with Jesus washing the disciples' feet. They continue with teaching that includes many beloved saying—about the vine and branches, the new commandment to love, the promise of the Spirit, among others.

John tells us that Jesus concluded this preparation with a threefold prayer (chapter 17)—for himself, for his immediate disciples, and for those who would come to believe.

When Jesus prayed for us future disciples, he asked for only one thing, but he asked it over and over. He repeated it three times, each time with increasing force:

- "...that they all may be one" (John 17:21);
- "...that they may be one as we are one" (John 17:22); and
- "...that they may be completely one so that the world may know that you have sent me and have loved them as you have loved me" (John 17:23).

Why did he offer that particular prayer? Was it because he saw this as both our greatest spiritual need and our greatest spiritual peril? Or was it because he saw that our spirit filled ability to live beyond our differences might be the most powerful witness to the power of the gospel of love? For whatever reason, that was the only prayer for us who would come to believe that John records in chapter 17.

That prayer still needs to be heeded today. People used to worry about too much church unity, about becoming "super churches" to the loss of important emphases and distinctives of various denominations. We are far from that now! Rather, we are more in danger of fragmenting and bickering ourselves into silence on the power of the gospel to confront the important issues that our society is facing.

What does Jesus's prayer mean for us, now, in this day with all of the needs and challenges that surround us? Desmond Tutu and the South Africans begin to answer this, but there is more. I invite us to open our spiritual eyes, to dream dreams, in short to activate our moral and spiritual imaginations. What might a reconciled-reconciling church, more attune to Jesus's prayer, be able to do in Christ's name?

I will offer a few responses to this question. Your dreams and hearts may take you much farther than I have yet been able to envision.

May We Be One in Living Obedience to Galatians 6:2

"Bear one another's burdens, and in this way you will fulfill the law of Christ."

I recall an experience of Christian unity far beyond my expectations. I had traveled to another city in order to take intensive training in "Stephen Ministry" so that I could begin this one-on-one lay ministry in my church. While I had read and heard good things about this program, expected excellent training, and knew it had originated in a Lutheran church, I had no idea of all I would experience during this training.

There were about four hundred of us who gathered for this equipping event, and we did indeed experience powerful worship, training and growth, community and friendship. I was told there were five from my denomination (American Baptist) there. I never found two of them, but it didn't matter. My best friends during those two weeks were Catholics from Detroit and Lutherans from Minnesota. My roommate was a Seventh Day Adventist from Hawaii. Two fine young Conservative Baptist pastors would visit with me from time to time about how to relate this program to our more casual, informal settings. Each day began with joyful worship including enthusiastic singing from both Protestant and Catholic songbooks and continued with in depth instruction and conversation.

I recall one incident of disharmony—when a staff member autocratically announced that future editions of a Stephen Ministry community agency guide would remove one agency because he did not like their stance on abortion. When several of us objected to him privately, he listened respectfully to what we had to say. I'm not sure what the outcome of that incident was. I still feel strongly about that, but it none of us allowed that conflict to block out our greater objective. We were all deeply committed to doing better at what we were instructed in Galatians 6:2 helping folks in our churches bear one another's burdens. This was a commitment we made for our churches, for the communities we served, and from church to church.

From my experience, this promise to be a caring network of churches of all denominations across the nation and world is a promise kept. Occasionally, I would receive notice from a person in another part of the country of someone who had come to our community and needed the care of a Stephen Minister (the term we used for those who had completed the training).[7] I willingly met this need by sending a Stephen Minister to the identified person to provide care for as long as needed.

Likewise, at least twice I made urgent calls to ministries in other parts of the country. Once, a man I knew was facing heart surgery alone. The other time, a lonely unmarried mother was undergoing chemotherapy far from home without the support of friends or family. In both situations, a Stephen Minister from a church in that community went to their side to offer care and support. I continue to feel enormous close-

---

7. The lay ministry program of which I was part was Stephen Ministries, 2045 Innerbelt Business Center Drive, St. Louis, MO 63114-5765, phone 314-428-2600.

ness to a church I see listed as a Stephen Ministry church and to persons who either render this service or have received it. We become one when we bear one another's burdens, and there are untold needs and opportunities for a caring, united church to reach out.

May We Be One in Embracing the Truth of Galatians 3:28

"There is no longer Jew or Greek, there is no longer slave or free, there is no longer male and female; for you are all one in Christ."

There is a barrier between Christian people that is too seldom breached—the boundary between believers who are of different races, ethnic groups, cultures. It is one of the scandals of the twenty-first century church that too little attention is given to this division of God's people.

Norman Anthony Peart aptly writes, "There is an *integral* link between racial reconciliation and spiritual reconciliation." Racial reconciliation should be seen as an outgrowth and an accentuation of the gospel's ministry. Peart offers three reasons why racial reconciliation should be connected to God's saving work. First, God's action in already reaching out to all the peoples of the earth stands as a pattern for the actions of God's people. Second, we are called to live in the reality of God's action, not that of the tragically separated cultures around us. And third, "the gospel is evidenced and magnified by the actions of its adherents."[8]

When we attempt to live out Jesus's prayer that we be one, we may need to break out of our comfortable cultural and racial enclaves and be open to something different. This may begin with interethnic and intercultural dialogue with persons and groups we have not engaged in depth before.

And this step, in turn, may require that we will have to shed some assumptions of being a superior culture and enter with humility into the conversation. Eric Law writes a dialogue is "an interchange of thoughts, feelings, and beliefs on a common subject between two or more persons of differing views." He points out that the most basic purpose of such a dialogue process is for "each person to learn from the other so that he or she can change and grow."

When persons take the risk and enter openly in such a process, some sort of multicultural community may begin to emerge. Law notes,

---

8. Norman Anthony Peart, *Separate No More: Understanding and Developing Racial Reconciliation in Your Church*, 105.

"A multicultural community . . . is not a melting pot, but a dynamic process in which the various cultural groups maintain their identities while engaging themselves in a constructive dialogue with each other. A true multicultural community seeks to maintain a balance of power, communication, and authenticity among the different cultural groups. No one group in this dynamic process will dominate, nor will any be made disadvantaged."[9]

Law works with communities that have need for persons with some cultural variations to understand each other better and deal with each other more effectively. These cultural differences may include race but not always. There may also be need to dialogue across language differences.

But there are other factors that contribute to a person's culture, such as gender, age, physical ability, economic status, religion, marital status, education, community, work, and family structure. Differences in any of these can occasion the need for multicultural dialogue. For example, persons of different generations may need such a dialogue over worship styles with particular attention to the music that speaks to each in worship.

Eric Law holds forth both the vision and the means for arriving at what he terms "the level ground of ethnorelativism where cultural differences are neither good nor bad but only different."[10] He makes clear that it is hard work to arrive at this place, and even harder work to stay there! It can also be an unbelievably beautiful place, for finally—at least in brief glimpses—we see the reality of Galatians 3:28, where race, privilege, gender do not matter for we are all one in Christ Jesus.

Sometimes this may lead to interracial and interethnic churches where many languages are spoken. Sometimes it will not. The Black church was first created out of necessity and has long been a vital force in developing leadership, providing community, and giving prophetic voice to justice issues. That precious heritage need not be lost even as we seek a greater unity than we have yet known.

We can start with stronger unions between churches, more conversation and dialogue, sensitivity to the justice issues each group is enduring, and commitment to the better treatment of all God's people. We can visit each other's churches and host each other in our homes. There can be interchurch dialogue groups.

9. Eric H. F. Law, *The Bush Was Blazing, But Not Consumed*, x.
10. Ibid., 61.

We can engage in joint mission projects together. (I am aware of two churches, one predominantly black, the other predominantly white that together built a Habitat for Humanity home.) We can discover the justice issues where our concerns converge and can work together on such justice issues. In my city, a coalition of churches of many ethnic groups exert moral leadership and pressure in such areas as fair hiring practices on public projects, more adequate mass transportation, and improved school systems.

We can mutually explore each other's history, the heroes and heroines of faith we admire, and the convictions that have emerged. We can learn from each other's wisdom and be enriched by each other's vitality.

I rejoice to be part of a seminary community that is richly interracial, inter-ethnic, inter-cultural, and international. In our chapel services, we frequently observe the Lord's Supper, often by walking forward to receive the communion elements. On those days, I love to sit on the aisle and pray for each person as s/he walks by, celebrating—in our small community—the rich diversity of God's family. I am so enriched by the mutual prayers, love, and respect of others in this community. There is so much more I have to learn from others whose history is different from my own, but I am growing. For that I give thanks.

Out of this, friendships can emerge, and, in addition, a mighty united stance of God's people. And, perhaps, there will be fervent prayers that the oneness of God's people will be even more deeply known.

I write these words shortly after the inauguration of Barack Obama as our forty-fourth president. In the wondrously joyous celebration, two themes were sounded over and again. One was that this was the beginning of the fulfillment of Martin Luther King's dream; that many African American children and youths would begin to believe that their possible futures were vaster than they previously imagined. The other was sometime soon that we won't think of him as our African American president, but as our president. That may lead in turn to seeing each other much more richly than simply viewing us in racial categories.

If our dynamic president can lead our nation into a "post-racial" era, surely the churches should not be far behind!

May We Be One in Obeying Jesus' Words in Luke 4 and Matthew 25

In addition to John 17, there are two more foundational passages that speak to what a reconciled and reconciling church should do and be.

In Luke 4, we read that Jesus worshipped in the synagogue in his hometown of Nazareth. When asked to do so, he read to them out of the scroll of Isaiah. This is what he chose to read:

> "The Spirit of the Lord is upon me,
> because he has anointed me to preach good news to the poor.
> He has sent me to proclaim release to the captives
> and recovery of sight to the blind,
> to let the oppressed go free,
> to proclaim the year of the Lord's favor." (Luke 4:18–19)

And then he told them, "Today this scripture has been fulfilled in your hearing." (v.21) This is Luke's description of how Jesus began his ministry after his baptism and the temptation in the wilderness.

Matthew (in chapter 25) includes words from Jesus near the end of his ministry on earth. At the end time, those who are blessed will be told,

> "I was hungry and you gave me food, I was thirsty and you gave me something to drink, I was a stranger and you welcomed me, I was naked and you gave me clothing, I was sick and you took care of me, I was in prison and you visited me." (Matt 25:35–36)

When the righteous blessed ones disclaim that they never saw the Son of Man in such circumstances, he will respond,

> "Truly, I tell you, just as you did it to one of the least of these who are members of my family, you did it to me."(Matt 25:40)

In the first of these two scripture passages, Jesus states his mission; in the second, he describes actions of people that will be honored when present and judged when such actions are absent. These scriptures offer a combined list of many things Jesus asks of his followers.

We are called upon to be advocates for the poor of the world and to bring about the release of captives. We are to resist the bondage of all oppressed people and contribute to the healing of those blind and the many that are sick with other infirmities. We are to respond to raw human needs such has hunger, thirst, lack of clothing, and the loneliness of being stranger. And we are not to forget those in prison.

What an agenda for God's united people! How touched we are to learn of people who are obeying Christ's radical commands in basic and simple ways. The whole world was moved by the life and example of

Mother Teresa and the many who joined her order to minister to the dying among the poorest of the poor. There are also many other lesser-known Christian people offering response to suffering as well. For example, I greatly admire Dr. Lewis Wall, a Washington University professor of obstetrics-urogynecology. Lewis has been concerned for the thousands of African women who, when delivering their babies far from medical care sometimes with long term labor, frequently suffer internal damage. A fistula (hole) between vagina and bladder may be the result, causing them to lose bladder control. As a result, they are ostracized by husband and community. Lewis has worked with doctors and facilities on both continents to marshal a response to this need—surgeries, clinics, the training of others in the surgical procedures, expanded hospitals. How moving is this response—and how much more help is needed to accomplish it!

Consider another example. In Nicaragua, one of the poorest countries of the world, there are numerous isolated villages with no medical care, educational facilities or any other infrastructure. In response to this crying need, committed Christian people have created an organization called Provadenic. If a community requests it, they will train a leader from that village in basic health, sanitation and community improvement methods and keep that person stocked with basic medicines. As a result, in a variety of villages, sanitation has improved, health has increased, and infant mortality has declined. This is another wonderful obeying of Christ's commands, and the needs are so far beyond their present resources.

As we look around at the many crying needs in our country and around the world, there is much that awaits the people of God, united in responding to Christ's mandates to us. Good health care, nutrition, and education for each of God's children all over the world; food for the hungry and homes for the homeless—these are a beginning. There are so many needs and so many ways to respond, ranging from one on one giving to large organizations, to lobbying our nation's leaders for systemic compassionate response. With room for all of us, united in obedience to Christ, we can minister to the least of these, his family members.

May We Be One in the Compassionate Anger of Jesus in Matthew 21:12–13

> Then Jesus entered the temple and drove out all who were selling and buying in the temple, and he overturned the tables of the money changers and the seats of those who sold doves. He said to them, "It is written,
>   'My house shall be called a house of prayer';
>   But you are making it a den of robbers."

While we have analyzed and refuted the "anger is sin" tradition, there is an opposite statement to be claimed. Sometimes, not to be angry is a sin! In this connection, Andrew Lester comments, "I believe . . . that *not being angry* at evil in all of its manifestations is sinful. In these circumstances, anger is a moral response."[11]

When we are confronted with injustice, when we see persons' worth, contribution or dignity denied, when we see persons suffering because of others' greed or indifference, anger is the most loving and the most Christian response! As ethicist Beverly Harrison has noted, "We must never lose touch with the fact that all serious human moral activity, especially action for social change, takes its bearings from the rising power of human anger."[12]

Of course, it will be necessary to find moral ways to express that anger. Mahatma Gandhi and Martin Luther King, Jr. pioneered in showing a way to channel the widespread and festering anger over colonialism and racism into significant confrontations, loving expression, and moral ends. Of course, theirs is not the only way, although it is one way that the world will never forget. All of us who are aroused by anger at injustice or suffering will need also to seek for many fitting ways to channel that anger.

At the same time, this shared anger may be a uniting force among people who have not worked together before. They are drawn together by urgency, by outrage, by the need to do something together. When this happens, Christian activists are wise to look for other common causes and other sources of Christian community with their newfound allies.

---

11. Andrew Lester, *The Angry Christian: A Theology for Care and Counseling*, 207.

12. "The Place of Anger in the Works of Love" in her collection of essays *Making the Connections: Essays in Feminist Social Ethics,* edited by Carol S. Robb, 14.

This is closely related to our discussion in the previous section. It may well be that our anger, because we care about something, is our way of perceiving our call to work on the justice and compassion issues of which we just spoke. May our compassionate anger lead us to others of similar convictions and may it propel us to persist in those just causes.

May We Be One in Reaching out to God's "Other Sheep" as Written in John 10:16

"I have other sheep that do not belong to this fold."

As I write this, our lives are filled with painful memories of terrorism and a constant wariness about it. Military leaders and diplomats puzzle how to deal constructively with the cultures of occupied regions, or how to encourage warring factions to reconcile. The world seems to grow not safer, but more dangerous. Prominent among those reasons for this is our lack of understanding of each other's cultures, including what offends and what stirs fear.

Part of the reason for such misunderstandings is the lack of effort toward dialogue and mutual conversation among peoples of the religions of those cultures. If, for years people of deep faith and spirituality had been carrying on dialogues with people of deep faith and spirituality in other religions, there might be more of a reservoir of understanding and good will. But we have not been doing that (at least not nearly enough of us), and now it is desperately needed.

I must confess I do not have as clear a biblical mandate for this claim on followers of Christ as there is for the others I mentioned. Ours is, after all, a missionary religion. For centuries, we have been acting on Jesus's command to "Go and make disciples of all nations." We do not abandon this even while we look for faithful ways to do this in a manner that is expressive of the love of God we have found in Christ. This calls us to be sensitive to and respectful of other cultures, including their religions. For any who are open, uncertain, disillusioned with their previous religion or having none, we are good news people with an invitation to walk a new way.

But there are many who are not searching for another religion. They are deeply rooted in a faith tradition, which they believe is based on God's revelation (just as we believe that about ours). Can it be that we can think of them as included in a word from Jesus? When he spoke about himself as the good shepherd, he included this sentence, "I have other sheep that do not belong to this fold" (John 10:16). This may be a way of seeing—that some seekers after God who do not share my Christian beliefs are God's other sheep.

If so, there will be no loss, and there may be immeasurable gain in respectful open-ended dialogue with them. We can learn of each other's spiritual search, beliefs, doctrines, and practices, what we hold in common, where we differ. A particularly fruitful conversation may be about spirituality and spiritual practices of each other's religious heritage. All that was said earlier about fruitful inter-cultural conversations certainly applies here as well.

Still another avenue might be to find those places of our common heritage. For example, at least two scholars, Bruce Feiler[13] and F. E. Peters,[14] have written studies on Abraham as a foundational source for Islam, Judaism, and Christianity. Such works might provide a fitting starting place for interfaith dialogue.

We can work together on issues of justice. We can model to leaders of governments that people of good will can live together on this earth that God has entrusted to us.

A united, renewed Christian church will have the inner strength and the power of its convictions to be able to carry on such conversations in the search for peace. What a gift that will be!

This is offered in a spirit of invitation and inquiry. A deeper Christian unity does not mean that we must totally agree on every aspect of the church's mission in that new day! There will be many open doors to service with the freedom to accept some and not others.

And there are so many more possibilities than I have mentioned. This is just a beginning to stir your moral imagination and spiritual leading. The greatest gift of this chapter may be not in what it suggests, but in what it stimulates you to dream, discover, and decide.

From the experiences I have had of the richness and power of God's reconciled people, I anticipate the greater realities we will see and the greater tasks we will achieve. How glorious it will be! I can hardly wait!

> *. . . And so, as did the great apostle Paul, I urge you to be of the same mind in the Lord. Loyal companions, who are not so directly involved in the issues, help those who are. For many of them have*

13. *Abraham—A Journey to the Heart of Three Faiths.*

14. *Children of Abraham: Judaism, Christianity, and Islam* and *Judaism, Christianity, and Islam: The Classical Texts and Their Interpretation.*

struggled for the gospel and their names are written in the book of life (Phil. 4:2-3).

"The grace of the Lord Jesus Christ be with your spirit"(Phil. 4:23). Amen!

QUESTIONS AND ACTIVITIES FOR GROUP REFLECTION

1. Someone might want to obtain a copy of Bishop Tutu's book, *No Future Without Forgiveness* and give your group a more thorough report of it. What stories of healing and forgiveness touched you most deeply? What are the discoveries you take from that book?

2. Why do you suppose that Jesus's prayer in John 17 included this thrice repeated petition "that they be one"? In what ways are you led to try to be part of the answer to that prayer?

3. When have you experienced times of richly meaningful oneness with God's people, either in one church or with persons from a variety of churches?

4. Which of the suggestions in this chapter—of ways a unified church could claim its mission—excited you most? What aspect of that suggestion stirred the greatest enthusiasm in you?

5. What other possibilities might you suggest as you think of the possible power and giftedness of a more deeply united church?

6. As we come to the end of this exploration, have someone read aloud to your group the letter at the beginning of this book. Then reflect in silence for a few minutes. What are you feeling? What do you think . . . about the thesis, the purpose for writing? At what points do you agree or question? What, if any, changes have you made while reading, reflecting, and discussing? What, if any, changes do you plan or hope to make in the future? May God richly bless your journey!

Resources for Congregations (and Other Entities) in Conflict

WHEN I TOLD YOU I would not provide a specific guide through the conflict process, I promised to provide you resources that do. While I have firsthand experience with some of the entities mentioned below, others were discovered through reading or recommendations of others. The listing here is, therefore, not an unqualified recommendation. Each person or congregation should do its own evaluation before engaging any of them.

AGENCIES

My first suggestion is to contact your denominational leaders in your area-region-diocese-Presbytery-judicatory. They may have persons to provide or may have recommendations about whom to contact and whom to avoid.

- The Consulting Office of Alban Institute. 2121 Cooperative Way, Suite 100, Herndon, VA 20171. Phone: 800-486-1318. Email: consult@alban.org. This agency works with religious organizations and has a nation wide network of consultants it can recommend.

- Association for Conflict Resolution. 1015 18th St. NW, Suite 1150, Washington, DC 20036. Phone: 202-667-9700. This is the professional society of conflict mediators working in many sectors, of which religion is one small part. They have an online directory that will provide names and brief information of consultants who might match your need.

- Lombard Mennonite Peace Center, 101 W 22nd St., Suite 206, Lombard, IL 60148. Phone: 630-627-0507. Email: admin@LMPeacecenter.org. Website: http://www.LMPeacecenter.org.

- Ron L. Claassen, Fresno Pacific University, Center for Peacemaking, 1717 S. Chestnut, Fresno, CA 93702. Phone: 559-453-2000. Email: rrclaassen@juno.com. Website: http://fresno.edu/dept/pacs/.

AGENCIES WITH RELATED SERVICES

These agencies—both mentioned in chapter 7—do not provide direct conflict management consultation but do provide helpful resources for a congregation seeking a richer community life.

- Water in the Desert Ministries, P. O. Box 65818, Albuquerque, NM 87193. Phone: 505-899-3738. Email: h20inthedesert@aol.com. Website: www.waterinthedesert.org. This ministry was entrusted with the trade mark and ongoing ministry for Worshipful-Work and develops materials and conducts training on discernment.
- Plowshares Institute. P. O. Box 243, Simsbury, CT 06070. Phone 860-651-4305. Email: plowshares@plowsharesinstitute.org. Website: www.plowsharesinstitute.org. They provide Community Conflict Transformation training events, manuals, and a video-tape, all useful for churches building up their own inner resources.

BOOKS

Three authors, within the longer bibliography that follows, offer specific and detailed guidance for churches experiencing conflict.

1. Hugh Halverstadt's *Managing Church Conflict* offers guidance, assuming that a church itself can take these steps.
2. Speed Leas's several books also offer detailed guidance. Leas also has a web site—just type in his name—that speaks of his availability as a consultant. The site lists his address as Box 2250, Boulder Creek, CA. Phone: 831-338-1025.
3. George W. Bullard, Jr., author of *Every Church Needs a Little Conflict,* provides guidance through a variety of levels of church conflict and also lists training opportunities in conflict management through The Columbia Partnership, 332 Valley Springs Road, Columbia, SC 29223-6934. Phone: 803-622-0923. Email: client.care@thecolumbiapartnership.org or GBullard@thecolumbiapartnership.org.

Bibliography

Achtemeier, Paul J. *The Quest for Unity in the New Testament Church*. Philadelphia: Fortress Press, 1987.
Augsburger, David W. *Anger and Assertiveness in Pastoral Care*. Philadelphia: Fortress Press, 1979.
———. *Conflict Mediation Across Cultures*. Louisville: Westminster John Knox Press, 1992.
———. *Hate-Work: Working Through The Pain and Pleasures of Hate*. Louisville: Westminster John Knox Press, 2004.
———. *The Love Fight: Caring Enough to Confront*. Scottdale, PA: Herald Press, 1973.
———. *When Caring Is Not Enough*. Scottdale, PA: Herald Press, 1983.
Bach, George R. and Peter Wyden. *The Intimate Enemy*. New York: Avon Books, 1968.
Barth, Karl. *The Word of God and the Word of Men*.
Bartlett, David. *Ministry in the New Testament*. Minneapolis: Fortress, 1993.
Bass, Dorothy, ed. *Practicing Our Faith: A Way of Life for Searching People*. San Francisco: Jossey-Bass, 1997.
Battle, Michael. *Reconciliation: The Ubuntu Theology of Desmond Tutu*. Cleveland: The Pilgrim Press, 1997.
Bixby, Douglas J. *Challenging The Church Monster: From Conflict to Community*. Cleveland: Pilgrim Press, 2002.
Boers, Arthur Paul. *Never Call Them Jerks: Healthy Responses to Difficult Behavior*. Bethesda: Alban, 1999.
Becker, Penny Edgell. *Congregations in Conflict: Cultural Models of Local Religious Life*. Cambridge: Cambridge University Press, 1999.
Birch, Bruce C., and Larry Rasmussen. *Bible and Ethics in the Christian Life*. Minneapolis: Augsburg, 1976.
Bradshaw, John. *The Family*. Deerfield Beach, FL: Health Communications, 1988.
Brueggemann, Walter. "Biblical Authority: A Personal Reflection." *Christian Century* (January 3–10, 2001) 14–20.
Buechner, Frederick. *Wishful Thinking*. New York: Harper and Row, 1972.
Bullard, George W., Jr. *Every Congregation Needs a Little Conflict*. St. Louis: Chalice, 2008.
Burtness, James H. *Consequences*. Minneapolis: Augsburg Fortress, 1999.
———. "When Christians Disagree." *The Lutheran* (August 9, 1989).
Bush, Robert A. Baruch, and Joseph P. Folger. *The Promise of Mediation*. San Francisco: Jossey-Bass, 1994.
Buttry, Daniel. *A Bible Study Manual on Conflict Transformation*. Self published and undated.
———. *Christian Peacemaking: From Heritage to Hope*. Valley Forge: Judson, 1994.
———. *Peace Ministry*. Valley Forge: Judson, 1995.

Carter, Stephen L. *Civility: Manners, Morals, and the Etiquette of Democracy*. New York: Basic Books, 1998.

Childs, Brevard. *Biblical Theology in Crisis*. Philadelphia: The Westminster Press, 1970.

Coser, Lewis. *The Functions of Social Conflict*. New York: Free Press, distributed by Simon and Schuster, 1964.

Cosgrove, Charles H., and Dennis D. Hatfield. *Church Conflict: The Hidden Systems Behind the Fights*. Nashville: Abingdon, 1994.

Delloff, Linda-Marie. "Congregational Conflict in Context." *In Trust* (Autumn 2000) 22–25.

Duff, Nancy. "How to Discuss Moral Issues Surrounding Homosexuality When You Know You Are Right." In Choon-Leong Seow. *Homosexuality and Christian Community*. Westminster John Knox Press, 1996.

Dunn, Larry A. "Transforming Identity in Conflict." In *Making Peace with Conflict*, edited by Carolyn Schrock-Shenk and Lawrence Ressler. Scottsdale, PA: Herald Press, 1999.

Evans, Alice Frazer, and Robert A. Evans with Ronald S. Kraybill. *Peace Skills: Leader's Guide*. San Francisco: Jossey-Bass, 2001.

Evans, C. F. "Peace." In Alan Richardson, *A Theological Wordbook of the Bible*. New York: The MacMillan Company, 1951.

Feiler, Bruce. *Abraham: A Journey to the Heart of Three Faiths*. New York: Harper Perennial, 2005.

Ferris, Theodore. "Exposition on Acts." In *The Interpreter's Bible, Volume 9,* edited by George Buttrick. Nashville: Abingdon, 1957.

Fisher, Roger and William Ury. *Getting to Yes*. Audiotape: New York: Simon and Schuster, 1987.

Frankena, William K. *Ethics*. Englewood Cliffs: Prentice-Hall, Inc., 1973.

Friedman, Edwin H. *Generation to Generation: Family Process in Church and Synagogue*. New York: The Guildford Press, 1985.

Gilmour, S. Maclean. *The Gospel Jesus Preached*. Philadelphia: Westminster, 1957.

Good, Dierdre. "The New Testament and Homosexuality: Are We Getting Anywhere?" *Religious Studies Review*. 26:4 (October 2000) 307–11.

Goleman, Daniel. *Emotional Intelligence*. New York: Bantam Books, 1995.

Gottman, John, and Nan Silver. *Seven Principles for Making Marriage Work*. New York: Crown Publishers, 1990.

Grenz, Stanley. *Welcoming but Not Affirming*. Louisville: Westminster John Knox Press, 1998.

Halverstadt, Hugh F. *Managing Church Conflict*. Louisville: Westminster/John Knox Press, 1991.

Harrison, Beverly Wildung. *Making the Connections*, edited by Carol S. Robb. Boston: Beacon Press, 1985.

Haugk, Kenneth C. *Antagonists in the Church*. Minneapolis: Augsburg, 1988.

Hays, Richard B. *The Moral Vision of the New Testament*. San Francisco: Harper San Francisco, 1996.

Heitler, Susan. *The Power of Two*. Oakland: New Harbinger Publications, Inc., 1997.

Hinman, Laurence. *Contemporary Moral Issues: Diversity and Consensus*. Upper Saddle River, NJ: Prentice-Hall, 1996.

Hollinger, Dennis P. *Choosing the Good: Christian Ethics in a Complex World*. Grand Rapids: Baker Academic, 2002.

Hopewell, James. *Congregations, Stories, and Structures.* Philadelphia: Fortress, 1987.
Johnson, Barry. *Polarity Management: Identifying and Managing Unsolvable Problems.* Amherst: HRD Press, Inc., 1992.
Kaufmann, Adrienne, and Kate Harvey. "Substantive Dialogue: A Tool for Congregations to Deal with Potentially Divisive Issues Without Becoming Divided." No pages. Handout distributed to American Baptist Ministers Council, ABC-USA Biennial, June 1999.
Keizer, Garret. *The Enigma of Anger.* San Francisco: Jossey-Bass, 2002.
Kimball, Charles. *When Religion Becomes Evil.* San Francisco: Harper San Francisco, 2002.
Kraybill, Ronald S., with Robert A. Evans and Alice Frazer Evans. *Peace Skills: Manual for Community Mediators.* San Francisco: Jossey-Bass, 2001.
Kraybill, Ron, and Evelyn Wright. *The Little Book of Cool Tools for Hot Topics: Group Tools to Facilitate Meetings When Things are Hot.* Intercourse, PA: Good Books, 1996.
Kritek, Phyllis Beck. *Negotiating at an Uneven Table.* San Francisco: Jossey-Bass, 1994.
Law, Eric H. F. *The Bush Was Blazing but Not Consumed.* St. Louis: Chalice, 1996.
———. *Inclusion: Making Room for Grace.* St. Louis: Chalice, 2000.
———. *The Wolf Shall Dwell with the Lamb.* St. Louis: Chalice, 1993.
Leas, Speed B. *Leadership and Conflict.* Eugene, OR: Wipf and Stock, 1982.
———. *Moving Your Church through Conflict.* Bethesda, MD: Alban Institute, 1985.
———. *Should the Pastor Be Fired?* Bethesda, MD: Alban Institute, 1980.
Leas, Speed B., and Paul Kittlaus. *Church Fights: Managing Conflict in the Local Church.* Philadelphia: Westminster, 1973.
Lederach, John Paul. *The Journey Toward Reconciliation.* Scottsdale, PA: Herald Press, 1999.
———. *The Little Book of Conflict Transformation.* Intercourse, PA: Good Books, 2003.
Lerner, Harriet Goldhor. *The Dance of Anger.* New York: Harper and Row, 1985.
Lester, Andrew. *Coping with Your Anger: A Christian Guide.* Philadelphia: Westminster, 1982.
———. *The Angry Christian: A Theology for Care and Counseling.* Louisville: Westminster John Knox, 2003.
Lorde, Audre. *Sister Outsider.* Berkeley: Crossing Press, 1984.
Lustberg, Arch. *Controlling the Confrontation.* Audiotape. U.S. Chamber of Commerce, 1990.
Markman, Howard, Scott Stanley, and Susan L. Blumberg. *Fighting for Your Marriage.* San Francisco: Jossey-Bass, 1994.
Marty, Martin. *By Way of Response.* Nashville: Abingdon, 1981.
Matthewes-Green, Frederica. "Pro-Life-Pro-Choice: Can We Talk?" *Sojourners Magazine* 23:10 (December 1994–January 1995).
McBride, J. LeBron. *Spiritual Crisis: Surviving Trauma to the Soul.* New York: Haworth Pastoral Press, 1998.
McClure, Lynn. *Anger and Conflict in the Marketplace.* Manassas Park, VA: Impact Publications, 2000.
McKinney, Lora-Ellen. *Getting to Amen: Eight Strategies for Managing Conflict in the African American Church.* Valley Forge: Judson Press, 2005.
Merton, Thomas. *New Seeds of Contemplation.* New York: New Directions, 1961.

Miller, Herb. "What Causes Congregational Conflict?" "How Can We Reduce Conflict Damage?" *The Parish Paper: A Resource for Congregational Leaders.* 8:8–9 (February-March 2001).

Miller, Mary Day. "Facing Conflict in the Small Church." *The Christian Citizen: Voices for Biblical Justice.* Valley Forge, PA: American Baptist National Ministries, 2000.

Mollenkott, Virginia. *Men, Women, and the Bible.* Nashville: Abingdon, 1977.

Morris, Danny, and Charles M. Olsen. *Discerning God's Will Together.* Bethesda, MD: Alban Publications, 1997.

Morseth, Ellen. *Ritual and the Arts in Spiritual Discernment.* Kansas City, MO: Worshipful Work, 1999.

Mouw, Richard J. *Uncommon Decency: Christian Civility in an Uncivil World.* Downers Grove: Intervarsity, 1992.

Mullen, Thomas J. *The Dialogue Gap.* Nashville: Abingdon, 1969.

Myers, David. *The American Paradox: Spiritual Hunger in an Age of Plenty.* New Haven: Yale University Press, 2000.

National Association for Community Mediation. "Case Study: The Buffalo Coalition for Common Ground." No pages. Online: http://www.nafcm.org/Casepage.html.

Niebuhr, H. Richard. *Christ and Culture.* New York: Harper and Row, 1956.

———. *The Purpose of the Church and Its Ministry.* New York: Harper and Brothers, 1956.

Novaco, Raymond W. "Anger." In *Encyclopedia of Psychology*, 1.

Nouwen, Henri. *The Road to Peace*, edited by John Dear. Maryknoll: Orbis Books, 1998.

Olsen, Charles. *Transforming Church Boards into Communities of Spiritual Leaders.* Bethesda: Alban, 1995.

Peart, Norman Anthony. *Separate No More.* Grand Rapids: Baker Books, 2000.

Peck, M. Scott. *A Different Drum: Community Making and Peace.* New York: Simon and Schuster, Inc., 1987.

Peck, M. Scott. *A World Waiting to be Born.* New York: Bantam Books, 1993.

Peters, F. E. *Children of Abraham: Judaism, Christianity, and Islam.* 2d ed. Princeton: Princeton University Press, 2004.

———. *Judaism, Christianity, and Islam: The Classical Texts and Their Interpretation.* Princeton: Princeton University Press, 1990.

Rediger, G. Lloyd. *Clergy Killers.* Louisville: Westminster John Knox Press, 1997.

Richardson, Ronald W. *Creating a Healthier Church: Family Systems Theory, Leadership, and Congregational Life.* Minneapolis: Fortress Press, 1996.

Rubin, Theodore Isaac. *The Angry Book.* New York: Collier Books, 1969.

Saussy, Carroll. *The Gift of Anger: A Call to Faithful Action.* Louisville: Westminster John Knox Press, 1995.

Sawyer, David R. *Hope in Conflict: Discovering Wisdom in Congregational Turmoil.* Cleveland: Pilgrim Press, 2007.

Scanzoni, John. *Love and Negotiate.* Waco: Word Books, 1979.

Scholer, David M. "Unreasonable Thoughts on the State of Biblical Hermeneutics: Reflections of a New Testament Exegete." *American Baptist Quarterly* 2:2 (June 1983).

Schreiter, Robert J. *The Ministry of Reconciliation: Spirituality and Strategies.* Maryknoll: Orbis Books, 2002.

Schrock-Shenk, Carolyn, and Lawrence Ressler, eds. *Making Peace With Conflict: Practical Skills for Conflict Transformation.* Scottsdale, PA: Herald Press, 1999.

Search for Common Ground. "The Common Ground Network for Life and Choice." No pages. Online: http://www.sfcg.org/programmes/us/us_life.html.

Sizoo, Joseph. "Exposition on Joshua," *The Interpreter's Bible, Volume 2*, edited by George Buttrick. Nashville: Abingdon, 1953.

Slaikeu, Karl A. *When Push Comes to Shove: A Practical Guide for Mediating Disputes*. San Francisco: Jossey-Bass, 1996.

Stassen, Glen H., ed. *Capital Punishment: A Reader*. Cleveland: Pilgrim Press, 1998.

Steinke, Peter. *Healthy Congregations: A Systems Approach*. Bethesda: Alban, 1996.

Stevens, Edward. *Developing Moral Imagination*. Kansas City, MO: Sheed and Ward, 1997.

Stone, Howard. *Crisis Counseling*. Minneapolis: Fortress Press, 1999.

Stott, John R. W. *Balanced Christianity*. Downers Grove: InterVarsity, 1975.

Stutzman, Jim and Carolyn Schrock-Shenk, eds. *Mediation and Facilitation Training Manual: Foundations and Skills for Constructive Conflict Transformation*. Akron, PA: Mennonite Conciliation Service, 1997.

Tammeus, Bill. "Theologically Speaking, Humility Would Help Us All." *The Kansas City Star* (August 4, 2001) B7.

Tavris, Carol. *Anger: The Misunderstood Emotion*, rev. ed. New York: Simon and Schuster, 1989.

Thomas, Marlin E., ed. *Transforming Conflict in Your Church: A Practical Guide*. Scottdale, PA: Herald Press, 2002.

Throckmorton, Burton H., ed. *Gospel Parallels: A Comparison of the Synoptic Gospels*. 5th ed. Nashville: Thomas Nelson Publishers, 1992.

Tillman, William, Jr. "The Church's Response to Homosexuality: Biblical Models for the 21st Century." *Review and Expositor* 98:2 (Spring, 2001).

Tutu, Desmond. *No Future Without Forgiveness*. New York: Doubleday, 1999.

———. *The Rainbow People of God: The Making of a Peaceful Revolution*, edited by John Allen. New York: Doubleday Image Books, 1994.

Vanderhaar, Gerard A. *Beyond Violence: In the Spirit of the Non-Violent Christ*. Mystic, CT: Twenty-Third Publications/Bayard, 2000.

"Voices of 2001," *Christian Century*, December 19–26, 6.

Wallis, Jim. *Who Speaks for God?* New York: Delacorte Press, 1996.

Whitehead, James D., and Evelyn Eaton Whitehead. *Shadows of the Heart: A Spirituality of Negative Emotions*. New York: Crossroad, 1994.

Willimon, William H. "Under Fire," *Christian Century*. May 2, 2001, 6–7.

———. *Preaching About Conflict in the Local Church*. Philadelphia: The Westminster Press, 1987.

Wink, Walter, ed. *Homosexuality and Christian Faith*. Minneapolis: Fortress, 1999.

Wuthnow, Robert. *Christianity and Civil Society*. Valley Forge: Trinity Press International, 1996.

www.ingramcontent.com/pod-product-compliance
Lightning Source LLC
Chambersburg PA
CBHW071447150426
43191CB00008B/1262